Making a Meal of It

Making a Meal of It

Two thousand years of English cookery

ENGLISH HERITAGE

Published by English Heritage, NMRC, Kemble Drive, Swindon SN2 2GZ
www.english-heritage.org.uk

Copyright © English Heritage & Maggie Black, Peter Brears, Jane Renfrew
& Jennifer Stead, 2005

Based on the *Food & Cooking* booklets published in 1985

10 9 8 7 6 5 4 3 2 1

ISBN-10 1 85074 971 X
ISBN-13 978 1 85074 971 7

Product code 51132

A CIP catalogue for this book is available from the British Library

Edited by Julia Elliott
Designed by Pauline Hull
Printed by Bath Press

CONTENTS

'Take a red cock that is not too old and beat him to death'

Thus begins an 18th-century recipe recorded by one William Kitchiner. Kitchiner's instruction reflects a cruelty to animals intended for the table that was widespread in his day, carried out in the belief that it improved the quality of their meat. English cooking has seen many fads and fancies over the centuries, particularly among those who could afford to eat well. Look no further than the Romans' fondness for dormice – fattened in pots and stuffed with dormouse meat, no less – and you sense the beginnings of a determination to eat well, though not always in a way that we would recognise today.

English cooking was always, and continues to be, influenced by the availability of ingredients and the arrival of new ideas from across the globe. Hence the story of cookery is also a story of exploration, war, trade, technological and social revolution, plague, politics and economics. Those at the lower end of the social scale generally got a raw deal; disease and war in the 14th and 15th centuries left the poor to grub out roots for their supper. Hardly surprising, then, that access to food could also be a potent symbol of power. Many servants in the 14th-century complained about their ration of common coarse bread, claimed by their masters to be the best sustenance for manual workers; in reality they kept the better wheaten bread for themselves as a sign of their high status.

Food is undeniably influenced by fashion, in some ages more so than by the foodstuffs available. In the Middle Ages people largely ignored the relatively abundant fruit and vegetables that would have improved their diet, preferring instead to eat bread and meat. In the mid-16th century the potato was a novelty served in the richer households and several centuries would pass before it became the staple food it is today. When sugar arrived, however, it was adopted with gusto and the English dental profession has never looked back. The 17th century saw an abundance of recipe books and the art of entertaining flourished as the country finally shrugged off its medieval habits. The gentry entertained in lavish style and Continental recipes were eagerly adopted, though 18th-century visitors were still startled by the English love of meat. The growth of the middle class in Victoria's reign created a demand for ever-more varied foods; they ate well and bought most of their food rather than growing it themselves. The evolution of mass production impacted even on the diets of the poorest members of Victorian society, and the average Victorian larder soon contained many processed foods that we continue to use today.

Drawing together information first published in English Heritage's historic cookery series, *Making a Meal of It* details the ingredients, recipes, etiquette and trends that have influenced English food from Roman times to the dawn of the 20th century. For those with a strong sense of nostalgia – and a strong stomach – the second half of the book presents a selection of recipes from Roman, Medieval, Tudor, Stuart, Georgian and Victorian England.

The timeless quest for food

THE ROMAN OCCUPATION AND THE TASTE OF THE MEDITERRANEAN

When the Roman legions invaded Britain in AD 43 they gave its people access to a new world of sophisticated tastes. They introduced many items into the British diet which are still common today including game such as pheasants and fallow deer; they also brought many fruit- and nut-bearing trees into cultivation and a wide range of herbs and plants. Commodities that were a highly valued part of their diet at home – dates, wine, olive oil and pepper for example – were imported into Britain.

There are several sources of evidence to draw on to reconstruct the diet of Roman Britain. Firstly, there is the physical evidence of the bones, seeds and shells recovered during archaeological excavations. For example, at Silchester in Hampshire more than a million oyster shells were recovered: the Romans were so fond of oysters that the presence of large quantities of oyster shells almost always indicates the proximity of Roman sites. Then there is the literary evidence including letters written to their families by soldiers serving on Hadrian's Wall describing the sort of food available. One writer lists 'spice, goats' milk, salt, young pig, ham, corn, venison and flour' while another letter mentions vintage wine, Celtic beer, ordinary wine, fish sauce and pork fat. Other literary evidence is of a more general kind: the recipe book and a book on sauces written by M Gaius Apicius who lived in the 1st century; the agricultural treatises of Cato, Varro, Columella and Palladius; Pliny the Elder's great work on natural history, and the accounts of notable feasts such as Petronius's satirical description of Trimalchio's banquet. Finally there are illustrations of foods and dining scenes in wall paintings and mosaics, and hunting and banquet scenes depicted on pottery.

One of the main differences between Roman cooking and that of today is the Romans' use of a sauce known as *liquamen*, or *garum*. This was made from the fermented entrails of fish combined with liberal amounts of pepper and it seems to have had a flavour resembling anchovy essence. The Romans were extraordinarily fond of this sauce and used it in sweet as well as in savoury dishes. It was made in many different parts of the Roman Empire and several towns were specially renowned for their liquamen factories, especially Pompeii and Leptis Magna.

Liquamen was used with the shellfish so prized as food in Roman Britain. Oysters from the coast near Colchester, Essex, and Richborough, Kent, were famous and were even valued in Rome. They may well have been transported live in tanks to inland sites. Other shellfish found on Roman sites are periwinkles, mussels, whelks, cockles and scallops.

Sea fish were also popular: cod, ling, haddock, grey mullet, herring and sea bream were caught, probably using a line and barbed bronze hooks which have been found on excavation sites. Crabs and lobsters were caught and transported inshore. Whale bones found at Caerwent, Gwent, may indicate that the occasional stranded whale was also used for food.

Oysters – a valued part of the Roman diet.
Opposite The Romans were extremely partial to snails and shellfish and usually cooked them in a dark fish sauce called liquamen.

There is little evidence for the kinds of freshwater fish which were caught, but at Silchester eel, dace, perch, pike and carp have been discovered, together with bronze fish hooks – and the remains of frogs, which may also have been eaten.

The Romans were probably the first people to enclose tracts of land as game parks where they kept and hunted red, roe and fallow deer, wild boar and the bears that lived in the remoter parts of Wales and Scotland. The Roman poet, Martial, describes how some British bears were taken to Rome to take part in wild-beast shows. Hunting scenes depicted on Castor-ware pottery, made in the Nene Valley, show running figures of dogs, hares and deer in low relief. Game was eaten either roasted or boiled and served with highly flavoured sauces.

Large game were kept in parks and small game such as hares were kept in *leporia*, or hare gardens, attached to the villas of the more well-to-do Romans so that they would be quickly available when needed for the table. Even smaller animals were kept for food: dormice were confined in pottery vessels and fattened on a diet of acorns and chestnuts before being killed, stuffed with minced pork and dormice meat and then baked in the oven. So far there is little direct evidence for this practice in Britain though it was very common in other parts of the Empire.

Snails were another delicacy and were treated with equal care. The snails had to be kept on land entirely surrounded by water to prevent their escape and they were deliberately fed on milk, wine and spelt wheat. For their final fattening, they were kept in jars with air-holes and when ready for eating, they were fried in oil and served with liquamen mixed with wine. Snail shells have been found on many Romano-British villa sites, indicating that they were a popular food.

Animals used for food depicted on Romano-British objects:
Left Hare brooch, Lincoln; Bronze figure of a boar, Hounslow, London; Bull's head bucket-handle mount, Felmersham on Ouse, Bedfordshire; Bronze figure of a roped stag, Milber Down Fort, Devon;
Opposite Cockerel brooch, Brough Castle, Cumbria.

Wild fowl were also an important part of the Roman diet; at Silchester, swan, goose, wild duck, teal, widgeon, woodcock, plover, crane and stork appear to have been eaten. The larger wild fowl were hung for some days to tenderise them. The problem of removing the sinews from cranes was tackled by cooking them with their heads outside the water; when cooked, the birds were wrapped in a warm cloth and held tightly while the head was pulled off with all the sinews attached so that only the meat and bone remained. Roast barnacle goose, *cherneros*, was described by Pliny as the 'most sumptuous dish known to the Britons'.

However, the bird most usually found on Roman sites throughout Britain is the domestic fowl. There were apparently two varieties: one with small leg bones displaying the well-developed spur of the game cock and resembled the modern bantam; the other was the ordinary domestic hen. The other domestic bird was the goose, probably a variety of the grey lag goose. Boiled or roasted, geese were served with thick sauces and they were often given elaborately spiced stuffings. Both birds produced a steady supply of eggs which were also used in cooking.

The Romans practised intensive rearing of delicate birds in special enclosures. They introduced pheasants, peacocks and guinea fowl into Britain, and they may also have kept partridges in captivity as they did in Italy. Peacock meat was so tough that it could only be made palatable if the bird was killed at least a week in advance. The meat was then converted into rissoles which were stewed in broth to which a little honey and pepper was added after cooking. Wood pigeons were encouraged to roost in *columbaria*, man-made pigeon houses built in the form of high towers with niches inside where the birds could nest and

The boar was the emblem of the Twentieth Legion stationed on Hadrian's Wall. Pork was a prized meat for Roman soldiers.

breed. People living in towns may have had earthenware dovecotes built on the roofs of their houses as in the Mediterranean area today.

The arrival of the Romans brought new farming practices to Britain. In southern England Italian-style villas were built and new domestic animals were introduced. The treatises of successful landowners on the Continent were read and noted and the management of livestock became much more scientific. The main object was to secure a better supply of meat, though milk, dairy products, hides and wool were also important. The new farming methods included the improved feeding of livestock and the growing of turnips made a significant contribution to the winter fodder.

British cattle were exported to the Continent even before the Romans arrived. Beef appears to have been the preferred meat of Roman Britain and was supplied as the meat ration of the Roman garrison. Several breeds of cattle are represented in bones collected from Roman sites: the shorthorn *Bos longifrons*; the larger *Bos taurus*; and an even larger form similar in size to the wild white Chillingham cattle of Northumberland. Remains of oxen have also been discovered: the principal beast of burden, the ox provided milk, butter, cheese and meat for the diet as well as leather, bone, horn and glue. Most of the cattle found on the military sites in the north of England were of the shorthorn type and the animals were usually mature with their bones often split for the extraction of the marrow. At Silchester a deposit of 2,500 lower jaws of cattle was discovered, and at another place on the same site 60 cattle horn cores were found – both deposits may be the refuse from some industrial activities but they do show that cattle were available in quite large numbers. At Cirencester,

Gloucestershire, the discovery of pits filled with cut and sawn bones below a shop floor has suggested that it was in fact a butcher's shop. At the Roman villa at Bignor, West Sussex, there were stalls for 55 head of cattle and a byre for 12 yoke of oxen. When beef or veal was cooked, it was often sliced and then served up in an elaborate sauce.

Pigs were also plentiful, especially in the south and east of the country, as pork was prized by the Roman soldiers and lard was part of their daily rations. Roman farmers introduced the practice of keeping pigs in sties to fatten them up and sties have been found on two villa sites – Pitney, Somerset and Woolaston Pit, Gloucestershire. Sucking pig was roasted in the oven and then served with a thickened sauce flavoured with pepper, lovage, caraway, celery seeds, *asafoetida* root, rue, *liquamen*, wine must and olive oil. Sow's udder was mixed in a *patina* – a broad shallow dish – with fish, chicken meat and small birds.

Hams and bacons were recognised as two different meats and were either dry-salted or pickled in their own brine. According to Apicius, they were both first boiled with dried figs, then the ham was baked in a flour and oil paste while the bacon was ready to be served with a wine and pepper sauce. The soldiers on Hadrian's Wall and on the Antonine Wall also consumed a fair amount of mutton as large quantities of sheep bones were found at Corbridge, Yorkshire, and at Barr Hill, Strathclyde. The Romano-British sheep seem to have been of light build resembling the Soay sheep still found on St Kilda today. Sheep pens for 197 sheep have been found at Bignor Roman villa together with what appears to be a lambing enclosure. Two varieties of goats were also kept, probably for their milk as well as their meat. There is

Soay sheep, probably the most primitive breed in the world having remained virtually unchanged since prehistoric times.

some evidence that horse meat was also eaten, possibly in the form of sauces. At the site of the Roman city of Verulamium at St Albans, Hertfordshire, there is a deposit of aged horse bones which have been dismembered and stripped of their flesh.

It may have been the practice to salt the meat to preserve it for later use. Salt was obtained by boiling brine in an evaporating furnace and remains of this activity have been identified at Goldhanger, Essex; Dymchurch and Cooling in Kent; Canewdon, Essex; and in the Fens and on the Lincolnshire coast. Salt springs were probably also used at Droitwich, Worcestershire, and Middlewich in Cheshire.

There is no evidence that butter was used in cooking as the Romans were more accustomed to cooking with olive oil or lard. The chief milk product known to be used was cheese and pottery cheese strainers have been found on many Romano-British sites. Cream cheeses may have been made in the shallow bowls known as *mortaria*; milk could be left in such bowls to curdle, the whey then being poured off through a spout in the rim. The grits on the inner surface of the bowl would retain the curd-forming bacteria from one cheese-making day to the next and so there was no need to use rennet, herbs or old whey to set the milk working. Curd cheeses were flavoured with herbs.

Cheese would have been eaten on it own with bread and it was also added to other dishes. Hard cheeses were sometimes sliced into salads while softer curd cheeses were used in *patina* dishes, mixed with other meat or fish ingredients, hard-boiled eggs, nuts and seasonings.

Various forms of wheat were cultivated in Roman Britain. The old hulled varieties of emmer and einkorn wheat continued

'Trust no one unless you have eaten much salt with him.'

Marcus Tullius Cicero, 106-43 BC

Opposite A *mortarium* and other earthenware vessels of the type used in Roman cooking.

to be grown, together with an increasing amount of spelt wheat – probably to meet the corn tax, or *annona*. All these hulled wheats need special drying treatment to release their grains efficiently in threshing; corn-drying kilns often found on villa sites were used to parch the spikelets of hulled wheat before threshing and grinding. The naked forms of wheat – bread and club wheat – are also known from Roman Britain but in much smaller quantities. Much easier to process, these gave rise to the varieties of wheat which are cultivated today. Both the naked and hulled varieties of six-row barley were grown too, but to a lesser extent and it appears that barley was used as punishment rations for soldiers on Hadrian's Wall and as fodder for horses.

Barley may also have been used for brewing. Sprouted grains of wheat and rye were found together at Caerleon, Gwent, in a situation which strongly suggests that they were deliberately sprouted to make malt. The manufacture of beer consists of two processes: malting and fermentation. In the first, the starch in the grain is converted to sugar by the release of the enzyme diastase during the natural germination process. This is encouraged by spreading the grain thinly over a warm floor and giving it a circulation of air and moisture. When the sprouts reach the length of the grain (after a few days), the germination is stopped by giving the malt a mild roasting. The next stage is to steep the malt in water, then to boil the infusion, the wort, with herbs to give flavour. The fermentation takes place when yeast is added to the wort and the liquid is then drawn off and stored in tightly sealed bottles or barrels. Possible bases of brewing vats have been found at Silchester, and in a barn near a granary at Wilcote Roman villa in Oxfordshire.

The Romans made a number of different kinds of bread:

Autopyron: a coarse, dark mixture of bran with a little flour made for slaves and dogs.
Athletae: a bread mixed with soft curd cheese, but otherwise unleavened.
Buccellatum: a biscuit or dried bread given to the troops.
Artophites: a light leavened bread made from the best wheaten flour and baked in a mould. Loaves of this sort of bread were found carbonised in Modestus's ovens at Pompeii.

Cereal grains were used for baking and for making porridge and gruel. The chief Roman food was a kind of gruel called *pils* or *pulmentus* made from barley or spelt wheat which was roasted, pounded and cooked with water in a cauldron to produce a porridge similar to modern polenta. The Romans also made a wheat starch product called *amulum* which they used for thickening sauces in the same way that cornflour is used today. It was prepared by soaking wheat grains in fresh water in wooden tubs and then straining the liquid through linen or wicker baskets before the grain turned sour. The liquid was poured on to a tiled floor spread with leaven and left to thicken in the sun.

The Romans were enthusiastic about vegetables. They grew peas and beans and imported lentils into Britain. They introduced many of the vegetable crops that are popular today such as cabbage, onion, leek, carrot, endive, globe artichoke, cucumber, marrow, asparagus, parsnip, radish and celery. They also ate a number of wild vegetable plants including nettles and pennycress.

Roman stone relief from the 2nd century AD depicting a bread seller.

As the Romans liked to enjoy their meat with an accompaniment of stuffings or sauces flavoured with herbs, it is not suprising that they introduced many new varieties into Britain to supplement the poppy seeds, mustard and coriander already known in prehistoric times. These new herbs included aniseed, borage, dill, fennel, garlic, lovage, mint, parsley, rosemary, rue, sage, savory, sweet marjoram and thyme. A shop selling herb seeds at Colchester, Essex, was burnt down during Boudicca's rebellion and the burnt seeds that survived include dill, coriander, aniseed, celery seed and poppy seed.

Honey was another popular flavouring and Columella and Palladius describe how wild swarms of bees could be trapped in empty hives placed near the places where they had been taking water. The colonies could then be installed in hives made from wood or withies on the farm.

Probably the most important fruit the Romans introduced into Britain was the grape. Grapes may have been imported in the form of raisins, sultanas or currants, sun-dried in the Mediterranean region, but they were also grown in southern England which was then the northernmost limit in Europe for ripening grapes. Direct evidence for the cultivation of vines comes from the finds of Sir John Evans in 1851 at Boxmoor villa in Hertfordshire where part of a vineyard with the vinestocks in position was discovered. Grape pips are often found on Roman sites and at Gloucester they were discovered together with grape skins and are thought to be the debris from winemaking.

The local wine was supplemented by imports of considerable quantities of wine-filled amphorae, first from Spain and then from south-west France. Wine from this area seems to have been

Filling up an amphora with wine in the door-to-door delivery service at Pompeii before its destruction in AD 63.

> 'Figs are restorative, and the best food that can be taken by those who are brought low by long sickness...professed wrestlers and champions were in times past fed with figs.'
>
> Pliny the Elder, AD 23–79

imported to Silchester in wooden barrels of silver fir, native to the Pyrenees. Wine was also imported from the Moselle region but ordinary or sour wine was the usual drink for soldiers on Hadrian's Wall. Wine merchants' shops have been identified at Verulamium, York and Lincoln, usually by the presence of a large number of broken amphorae.

If wine was intended for use in cooking, it was reduced by boiling before it was stored in order to concentrate its sugars and make it keep better. The boiled-down must, or *defructum*, was also added to sharp new wines to help them keep.

Vinegar was manufactured from wine which had gone flat, with additional yeast, salt and honey. It had many uses. Vinegar-sharpened sauces and dressings were popular and it was used in the preservation of fruits, vegetables and even fish as raw oysters were said to keep well if washed in it, as were pieces of fried fish if plunged into vinegar immediately after cooking. Vinegar also made a refreshing drink when diluted with water and was included in the rations for soldiers on the march. It is possible that *alegar*, a type of sour ale or malt vinegar, was also coming into use in Roman times.

Figs were another Roman introduction and may well have been grown in southern England. However, because the fruits which ripen here bear their fruit without pollination and so do not develop hard seeds, the figs identified by the presence of their seeds alone must have been imported to Britain from warmer climates.

Among the other orchard crops introduced at this time were the medlar, mulberry, damson, plum and cultivated cherry. Apples and pears were also being grown in orchards and there is ample

evidence that local wild fruits were used in season. Seeds of blackberry, raspberry, strawberry, crab apple, bullace and elder have been found at Silchester. Various nut-bearing trees were introduced at this time, including the walnut, almond and stone pine. The cones and kernels of the latter seem to have had a ritual as well as culinary significance.

In the 5th century AD the Roman armies gradually withdrew from Britain and the Roman government on the continent relinquished its hold over its far-flung province. But Roman influence would have survived long after the departure of Roman rule. Some sources believe that a Romano-British ruling class emerged in those towns that survived the Roman withdrawal. Though there is relatively little information about life in the 'Dark Ages' that followed, it is likely that Roman domestic habits survived, at least in urban areas, and Romano-British society is now known to have endured for centuries after the invasion and subsequent rule of the Anglo-Saxons.

MEDIEVAL ENGLAND – FOOD IN A FEUDAL SOCIETY

Knowledge of English medieval cooking has usually been gleaned from indirect sources such as government and church regulations, account and rent books, and a few books about table manners and diet. Pictures and poems like Chaucer's *Canterbury Tales* fill in further social detail. The earliest surviving English recipe book dates from about 1390 when *The Forme of Cury* was written by order of King Richard II.

Bread was everyone's staple food in the Middle Ages, but the grain it was made from varied from place to place and according to income. Wheat made the finest, whitest bread but, as it only grew on good soil, only the lord of the manor could afford to have land dug over and manured for it. The main types of white bread were:

Pandemain or **paynemaine**: the finest quality bread made from flour sifted two or three times.
Wastel: another first-quality bread made from well-sifted flour.
Cocket: a slightly cheaper white bread which was replaced around 1500 with small loaves or rolls of top-quality white bread called manchets (hand-sized breads).

The commonest bread, called maslin, mesclin or miscellin, was made from wheat and rye flour mixed together while darker

A medieval kitchen depicted on a Victorian stained-glass window at Spenfield Hall, Headingly, Leeds, West Yorkshire.

loaves were made from rye flour alone. Other breads included cheat, a wholewheat bread with the coarse bran removed, and tourte (or trete or treet), also known as 'brown bread', which contained husk as well as flour and may have been the bread used for trenchers (see below). Barley and oats were the breadcorns of northern and western regions where the climate was wet and cold, and these were made into barley bread and oatcakes, which are still called havercakes or clapbread. Weed seeds were nearly always included in any grain and, when the harvest was poor, beans, peas and even acorns were used in the cheapest bread, known as horse bread.

Better-off people used brown bread as trenchers – plates made by cutting large loaves, preferably four days old, into thick slices with a slight hollow in the centre. An ordinary person would have only one or two plate trenchers for a whole meal but the lord of the manor would have several stacked up for him. Leftover trenchers were gathered up in a basket and given to the poor after the meal.

Plain toasted bread was used a great deal in cooked dishes, and breadcrumbs were a standard way of thickening sauces and stiffening custards. Gingerbread was simply a heavily spiced breadcrumb-and-honey mixture often decorated with box leaves stuck on with whole cloves. Other cakes and buns were just sweetened, spiced pieces of bread dough.

Fish was almost as important as bread in the medieval diet. The Roman Catholic Church, to which everyone belonged, dictated that on Fridays (and until late in the period, Saturdays and Wednesdays) no one should eat meat. During Lent it was also forbidden to eat eggs and other dairy foods which meant that for

Most country people baked their own bread but in the towns professional bakers operated and were notorious as crafty swindlers. To counteract their dishonesty, a set of regulations for assessing bread prices was laid down in 1267 by royal order. Called the Assize of Bread, it tried to make sure that everyone paid a fair price for a loaf and no more. It was difficult to enforce, especially in small rural markets, but bakers who were caught flouting it were punished severely and it was at least a responsible attempt to see that ordinary people could afford a very basic product.

Poorer people had another grievance besides bread prices. By about 1350, servants and serfs were complaining that they were only issued with coarse maslin or brown bread, and free labourers also resented not getting wheaten bread. Their masters justified it by saying that branny brown bread sustained those who did heavy manual work for long hours, but that it caused wind in people who lived sedentary lives. In fact, their real reason for reserving the wheaten bread for themselves was that it served as a status symbol.

A wide variety of fish was available to cater for all the 'fish days' in the year – but there were other, rather curious animals which were also classified as 'fish'. For instance, barnacle geese and puffins were alleged to be fish because they were said to be created at sea, while beavers, which still existed in medieval Britain, were said to have fishes' tails!

about half the days in the year everyone had to eat fish. Churchmen had even more restricted meals: officially, the Rule of St Benedict forbade 'the meat of quadrupeds' to monks except for the sick, but from the 13th century the dietary strictures were respected less and less and by the 15th century were usually honoured only at formal banquets.

For ordinary people, fish meant salted or pickled herrings. England's herring fleet caught thousands of fish throughout the summer and there was a big salting and pickling industry to process them for transport inland. Apart from dried cod, called 'stockfish', which was as hard as board, poor people inland got no other sea fish. Londoners and people living near the east coast were luckier because they could get oysters and whelks quite cheaply.

The wealthy had a wider choice of sea fish, including many well known today, such as plaice, haddock and mackerel, as well as more exotic ones. Seals were eaten and so were the so-called 'royal' fish – whale, sturgeon and porpoise; these belonged to the king though in practice he often gave them away. Shellfish such as crab and lobster were common and popular.

In summer, when Lent was past, ordinary people inland could vary their diet by catching river fish and collecting eels. Landowners enjoyed plentiful supplies of river fish such as salmon, trout, grayling, bream and tench. Most estates of any size also had their own fishponds, called 'stews', in which they bred carp (a luxury) and pike (fairly common). Pickled salmon was a luxury imported from Scotland and Ireland when out of season. Since so much salt fish had to be eaten, many spice and herb sauces were developed specially to serve with them. Fried parsley was already a favourite garnish for fish.

The Normans gave sheep-meat the name of mutton (from *mouton*, the French word for sheep). It was second favourite to beef at this time but both these red meats were preferred to the white meats of veal and kid as they made more solid, satisfying roasts. Goats were also kept for milk and meat.

A pig was a poor man's standby because it could forage for itself year-round in the woods and fight off most foes. It looked and behaved like a wild pig but its flesh made good pickling pork or bacon, the poor man's only winter meat. The 'innards' made blood puddings and other sausages and the fat could be eaten on bread or used for cooking.

Cattle, sheep and goats, unlike swine, could not feed themselves throughout the winter and so fodder was a constant problem. As a result, all beasts except breeding stock and milk animals were slaughtered at intervals throughout the winter to provide fresh offal and salted joints. Beef sides, or goat and mutton hams, were salted and smoked like pork. Fresh mutton could be roasted if young but was better boiled if elderly. All domesticated animals were small, scrubby creatures, very different from and much less meaty than today's specially-bred animals.

After the Norman Conquest, game animals were designated the personal property of kings and nobles and poachers were mutilated or executed if caught. But although hunting wild bull, boar and deer remained an aristocratic privilege, hares and adult rabbits, which were called 'coneys', were made poor men's prey and free meat at the beginning of the 13th century. Wild cattle were becoming rare,

A 15th-century misericord at St Laurence's Church in Ludlow, Shropshire, showing a man enjoying a bowl of soup in front of a roaring fire. A cooking pot simmers on the logs and two large hams (or possibly containers made from animal skins) hang from a beam.

but boars were common almost until Tudor times and provided traditional Christmas brawn for all large feudal households. Roasting cuts of venison and pasties were 'top table' fare, but 'umbles' (liver and lungs) made pies for the huntsmen and the lower tables at a household feast.

Poultry, game birds, small birds and waterfowl were enjoyed by everyone, especially the clergy, who were officially allowed to eat 'two-legged' but not 'four-legged' meat. As well as hunting wildfowl with falcons, a noble household would employ its own bird-catcher or bargain with a local poulterer for supplies, and would also have its own dovecote and domestic poultry yard (for pheasants and partridges as well as hens, ducks and geese). Some of this backyard stock might be cooped and fattened – battery rearing and force-feeding were common. Even the poor kept chickens but, as eggs were so precious, they would prefer to catch a wild bird to eat rather than kill their own hens.

The types of bird eaten in the Middle Ages were far more varied than those of today. A swan or peacock was served at a banquet or celebration, dressed up as a processional centrepiece for the top table. Bustard were also served at parties; these enormous birds could weigh up to 12 kilos (25 lbs) and could hardly fly. Other unusual meat choices were crane, heron (especially the young called 'heronshewes'), gull, curlew, egret, quail, plover, snipe, blackbird (the most expensive of the small birds), lapwing, thrush, bittern and greenfinch. Dishes of birds like these were served at almost all well-to-do meals, lay or clerical. At a feast there might be as many as 20 dishes of them.

The milk of cows, sheep and goats was used throughout the Middle Ages, though cow's milk became more popular in the late

14th century because it was less work to milk one cow than ten sheep. Milk, cream, butter and cheese, together with eggs, were called 'white meats'. On large feudal estates, the milk was turned into cream, curds, soft cheese and butter for the lord's kitchen, and the residual whey and buttermilk made hard, skim-milk cheese for the servants and workers. This skim-milk cheese was sometimes so hard that it had to be soaked and then beaten with a hammer before it could be eaten!

Well-to-do adults thought fresh milk was a drink only fit for children, the old and invalids, though they enjoyed thick rich cream and curdled cream. They also thought butter was unwholesome for grown men to eat from midday onward, but children got bread and butter for breakfast and supper. However, cooked dairy foods were another matter. Milk made hot drinks called 'possets' or 'caudles' as well as cream soups and delicious custards. Cream made even richer ones. Soft, rich cream cheese called 'ruayn' or 'rewain' cheese made cheesecakes much like modern ones to supplement the rich man's meat dishes.

Even a medieval peasant kept a cow if he could, and unlike his lord he relied on it for food. Curds and whey, buttermilk, heavily salted butter and cheese were his staples. In summer he made soft cheese called 'spermyse' or 'green cheese'. Bread, and hard skim-milk cheese which kept all winter, were his daily diet in the fields as he ploughed, sowed and harvested the vital breadcorn.

Sheep were a valuable source of food as they provided both meat and milk.

In the Middle Ages everyone, high or low, ate pottage daily. This was broth or stock in which meat and/or vegetables had been boiled along with chopped meat, herbs and very often cereals or pulses. The result was a soup-stew rather like Scotch broth. The pottage might be thick ('running') or almost thick enough to slice ('stondyng'). One well-known thick cereal pottage was 'frumenty' which consisted of hulled wheat boiled in milk and seasoned with cinnamon; other thick, more luxurious pottages were called 'mortrews'. A peasant made do with pease pottage which was rather like runny pease pudding.

The commonest pottages, however, were vegetable ones, made with red or green cabbages, lettuces, leeks, onions and garlic. Leek pottage, or 'white porray' as it was called, was especially popular and during Lent the rich ate it thickened with ground almonds. Green porray, made with green vegetables and flavoured with parsley and other herbs, was also eaten a great deal. A green herb pottage simmering over the fire must have smelt delicious but, sadly, it was probably over-boiled and not very nourishing. Various kinds of roots from the garden might be added to pottage, such as turnips, carrots and rape (now only a field crop for oil); potatoes, of course, were not known at this period.

Any medieval garden contained a wide variety of 'pot-herbs' (vegetables 'for the pot') and herbs used for flavouring and as medicines. Salad vegetables also had an important place in the garden. One attractive idea, which has become popular once again, was the use of primroses, violets and borage flowers in salads. Fruit and roots were frequently pickled and added as well.

Apples and pears, including the large, hard pears called 'wardens', were usually cooked rather than eaten raw. 'Roasted'

The vibrant hues of borage flowers made an attractive decoration for salads.

(baked) apples were very popular. Citrus fruits began to be imported around 1290 and lemons and Seville oranges were used both fresh and pickled, though both were very expensive. At first, sweet lemon preserves were bought from importers but English housewives soon learnt to make their own.

Other imports, reserved at first almost entirely for the rich because of their price, were currants, raisins, figs, dates and prunes. Dried fruit, together with spices, created the character of typical medieval feast food. Dishes for the wealthy were full of them and poorer people generally got some at Christmas and on feast-days.

The biggest luxury import was almonds. On fast-days, ground almonds could be substituted for pounded chicken as a thickening or diluted to make a substitute for cow's milk. Almond milk features in dozens of recipes. The poor had to make do with oatmeal but in season they could gather wild hazelnuts and cobs as a useful addition to their diet.

Cane sugar came to England with the Crusaders returning from the East some time before 1100. It was imported ready processed in the form of cones called 'loaves' – white if refined and fairly pure, otherwise a dirty brown. However, it was so rare and expensive even at the end of the Middle Ages that it was treated as a spice and kept under lock and key.

Salt had been mined in England since early times and was also made from evaporated sea water. Apart from the tons used for preserving, it was also a valued cooking spice. Mustard, like saffron, was also home-produced. Pepper was the only spice imported in large quantities and everyone, high and low, used a great deal of it.

Hazelnuts were used as a substitute for almonds in medieval times.

Not only was medieval food spiced, it was also highly scented and coloured. Jellies were set in different coloured layers for a striped effect, rice pudding was bi-coloured and custards were reddened. Saffron provided yellow, sandalwood red, parsley juice green, and turnsole (a violet-blue pigment derived from heliotrope or borage) purple. For a particularly ostentatious gift some foods, such as meatballs, were gilded with thin sheets of gold leaf.

Medieval people wanted more than just salt, pepper and mustard as condiments. Wealthy European cookery was aromatic and pungent with ginger, cinnamon, nutmeg, mace, cardamoms and cloves, and other spices we no longer use such as grains of paradise and cubebs. They were popular because they masked and improved the taste, not so much of tainted food (though they helped that too) but of the seemingly unending salted and dried winter foods. These were more expensive for the British than for anyone else because they were not imported in direct shipments but had to be bought from merchants who travelled to markets on the Continent.

Grocers also made up and sold ready-ground mixed spices to medieval housewives. The most usual mixtures were called 'powdor fort' and 'powdor douce'. Recipes varied, but powdor fort, which was 'hot', generally included ginger, pepper, and mace, and sometimes dried chives, while the gentler powdor douce contained ginger or cinnamon, nutmeg, a little black pepper and sugar, and sometimes cloves.

Medieval cookery is often believed to have been thoroughly over-spiced and certainly some of it was. However, the number of spices used in a dish does not indicate how much of each was used, or their strength. Spices had been brought long distances by sea or overland in all weather and must often have lost some of their intensity by the time they arrived. Moreover, since they were so costly they were hardly likely to be used over-generously.

There were times of desperate famine in the Middle Ages. The Black Death in the mid 14th century left villages depopulated with few to till the soil or sow next year's grain. Local battles during the Wars of the Roses in the 15th century left the fields trampled, the livestock slaughtered or driven off, and the field-workers gone. The few people left grubbed roots from the ground, ate marsh plants and trapped small wild creatures to survive. Yet even a peasant had certain customary rights to land, grazing and food, which a wise lord respected and in better times would have had certain things of his own such as his cow and strip of land in the communal field. Nevertheless food resources in the Middle Ages were restricted, and some foods which could have helped them greatly – such as fresh fruits and vegetables – were largely ignored.

Spices such as cinnamon livened up the dried and salted winter food.

TUDOR ENGLAND AND THE FOODS OF THE WIDER WORLD

'Cookery is become
an art, a noble science;
cooks are gentlemen.'

Robert Burton, 1577–1640,
Anatomy of Melancholy

The colourful flowering of Tudor England has bequeathed to posterity a whole series of rich and potent images, full of spectacle and a robust joie de vivre. The paintings of Nicholas Hilliard and his contemporaries show the lavish and colourful dress of men and women who enjoyed the music of Morley, Dowland and Campion, the poetry of Spenser and Sidney, and the plays of Marlowe and Shakespeare. The houses they occupied, from the soaring honey-coloured splendours of Burghley, Hardwick and Longleat to a host of brick and half-timbered country manor houses, similarly evoke the essential spirit of this period. Most potent of all, however, are the portraits of Henry VIII and Elizabeth I, a Renaissance prince and a sacred virgin presiding over a new age of development and increasing trade. The magnificence of their costumes, the fabulous richness of their apartments, and the elaborate ceremonies of their courts were all essential elements in leading and controlling a country still divided into religious factions and under constant threat of insurrection or invasion.

Against this background, the cookery of the period similarly reflects the influence of Renaissance Europe, in addition to fuelling the sumptuous entertainments held largely for political reasons both at court and in the larger houses. A great variety of documentary sources, ranging from estate papers to plays and poems, refer to the preparation of food. However, it was Edward White and his fellow London publishers of the late 16th century who provided the most important and unique legacy of information by collecting and publishing a series of cookery books.

Though exotic foodstuffs began to arrive from the New World, in general the foods enjoyed in the 16th century were almost identical to those of the Middle Ages. The range and qualities of these foodstuffs are best described in the physician and author Andrew Boorde's *Compendyous Regyment or Dyetary of Health of 1542*, where he writes:

> *Beef is a good meate for an Englysshe man, so be it the beest be yonge, & that it be not kowe-fleshe; yf it be moderatly powdered [i.e. salted] that the groose blode by salt may be exhaustyd, it doth make an Englysshe man stronge; Veal is good and easily digested; Brawn [boar's meat] is an usual meate in winter amonges Englisshe men; Bacon is good for carters and plowmen, the whiche be ever labouringe in the earth or dung … I do say that coloppes [slices of bacon] and egges is as holsome for them as a talowe candell is good for a blereyed mare … Potage is not so moch used in al Crystendom as it is used in Englande. Potage is made of the lyquor in the which fleshe is soden [boiled] in, with puttyng-to chopped herbes and otemel and salt. Fyrmente is made of whete and mylke, in the whiche yf flesshe be soden … it doth nourysshe, and it doth strength a man. Of all nacyons and countres, England is beste servyed of Fysshe, not onely of al maner of see-fysshe, but also of fresshe-water fysshe, and al maner of sortes of salte-fysshe.*

Serving a raised pie.

Boorde also advised his readers to eat vegetables such as turnips, parsnips, carrots, onions, leeks, garlic and radishes and fruit in the form of mellow red apples. Even so, raw vegetables and fruit were regarded with great suspicion by most Tudor diners who felt they were likely to be the cause of sickness and disease. It was for this reason that the sale of fruit was banned in the streets during the plague of 1569. However, cooked fruit and vegetables gradually became more popular.

In addition to the apples, pears, plums, cherries and woodland strawberries which had been grown in Britain for centuries, new fruits from southern Europe were now introduced into the gardens of the wealthy. These included quinces, apricots, raspberries, redcurrants and blackcurrants, melons, and even pomegranates, oranges and lemons. The last were never really successful however and citrus fruits continued to be imported in large quantities to serve the luxury market.

As a result of the mid-16th-century exploitation by Spain of her great South American colonies, a number of rare and exotic vegetables slowly began to arrive in Elizabethan England. Tomatoes came from Mexico and kidney beans from Peru, for example, while the potato was introduced from Chile and the Andes. Centuries were to pass before the true value of these new foods was fully appreciated, however, and they continued to be served largely as unusual delicacies in the well-to-do households.

A much more popular introduction from the New World was the turkey, a native of Mexico and of Central America, which had already found its way on to English tables by the 1540s. One of the explorer Sebastian Cabot's commanders, Sir William Strickland of the East Riding of Yorkshire village of Boynton,

'Beware of green sallettes & rawe fruytes for they wyll make your soverayne seke.'

Boke of Kervynge, 1500

claimed to have brought the first turkeys into this country and therefore adopted a white turkey-cock with a black beak and red wattle as his family crest. Birds of this type were available in the London markets of the mid-16th century.

Probably the most important culinary development in the 16th century was the growing popularity of sugar. In addition to the well-established sources of supply in Morocco and Barbary, increasing quantities were coming into Europe from the new Portuguese and Spanish plantations in the West Indies, some arriving through the activities of British privateers. In the 1540s a refinery in London was built to carry out the final stages of purification, converting the coarse sugar into white crystalline cones weighing up to 7 kg (14 lbs). These were then used to prepare a great variety of sweetmeats, crystallised fruits, preserves and syrups, as well as seasoning for meat, fish and vegetable dishes.

The national annual consumption of sugar averaged no more than 450 g (1 lb) a head during this period, but the great majority of this was eaten by the aristocracy who rapidly began to suffer from tooth decay. As the German traveller Paul Hentzer noted, even Queen Elizabeth's teeth were black, 'a defect the English seem subject to, from their too great use of sugar'. The ashes of rosemary leaves or powdered alabaster rubbed over the teeth with the finger helped to prevent tooth decay, as did the use of elaborate toothpicks made of precious metals, often worn in the hat. Expert barbers also used metal instruments to scrape the teeth before applying aqua fortis (nitric acid) to bleach them. As the writer and inventor Sir Hugh Platt warned, this treatment could be disastrous, for after a few applications a lady may 'be forced to borrow a ranke of teeth to eat her dinner, unless her gums doe help her the better'.

DINING À LA MODE – 17th-CENTURY REFINEMENT

'It was a common saying among the Puritans, "Brown bread and the Gospel is good fare".'

Matthew Henry, 1662–1714, *Commentaries*

The 17th century was a period of tremendous upheaval and change. Virtually every aspect of national and domestic life was transformed as England cast off many of her medieval traditions to emerge as a new, forward-looking state. As a result of the Dissolution of the Monasteries in the 1530s, vast areas of land and previously untapped economic resources had passed into lay hands. As they were enthusiastically developed over the succeeding century, their growing productivity financed the rise of what was to be a new, prosperous and influential class – the landed gentry.

In an age when the sovereign sturdily maintained his Divine Right to govern as he wished, it was impossible for the gentry to obtain the political power they now sought. The resulting friction between these opposing views flared up into the Civil War that resulted in the execution of Charles I in 1649. After just a decade of puritanical Commonwealth government, England returned to monarchy with Charles II in 1660. However, it was now a constitutional monarchy that recognised the right of Parliament to play a leading role in managing the country's affairs.

These upheavals had a considerable effect on domestic life. From the early 1600s, the increasing affluence of the gentry had enabled them to spend much more on recreation, travel and luxury goods. Instead of living throughout the year on their quiet estates, they now spent long periods in the towns with visits to London allowing them to acquire all manner of social graces. In the 1620s, proclamations ordered the gentry to return to their estates to prevent the neglect of public duties, avoidance of tax and heavy expenditure on foreign luxuries and expensive foods. These were largely ignored, however, and lavish entertainment flourished during the London season, as the city continued to develop into the finest food market in the kingdom.

Up to this time the fare of the country gentleman had been relatively plain and simple, largely based on home-produced meat, game and grain, roasted, boiled or baked as required. Plenty had been preferred to variety, but now there was an increasing demand for new delicacies, with new flavours and new methods of cookery. As in all aspects of social life, the royal household set the standards of culinary taste, drawing both on its own centuries-old traditions and on developments from France. Dishes that appeared at court would be imitated in lesser households and thus proceed on down the social scale.

At parties ladies would exchange recipes for their own specialities together with those culled from the growing range of recipe books. Between 1600 and 1700 a new volume appeared almost every other year, the most popular of these often running into a number of editions. With titles such as *The English House-Wife, The Accomplisht Lady's Delight*,

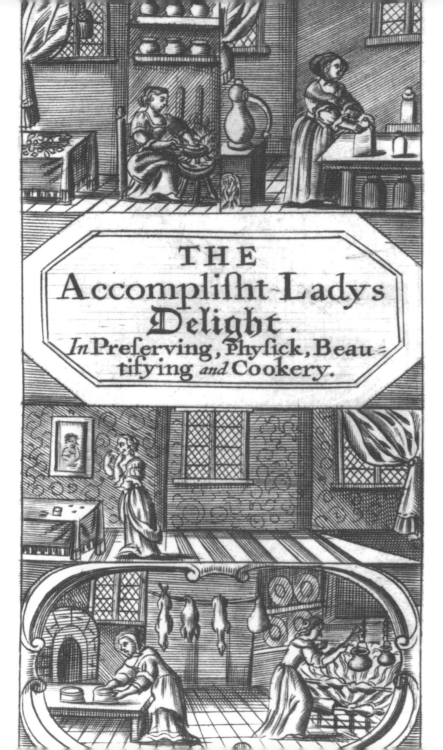

THE
Accomplisht Ladys
Delight.
In Preserving, Physick, Beau = tifying and Cookery.

Title page, 1675.

and *The Genteel House-Keeper's Pastime*, they appear to have been primarily intended for use in prosperous families where the lady of the house was responsible for all aspects of housekeeping. These volumes contained many items from overseas, such as 'a Persian Dish', 'a Turkish Dish', 'a Portugal Dish' or even 'an Outlandish Dish', but France provided the most fertile source of new recipes. In the late 16th century Sir Hugh Platt had published some 'after the French fashion' while John Murrell's *New Booke of Cookerie* of 1617 was 'all set forth according to the now new English and French Fashion'.

F P de La Varenne's *Cuisinier François*, published in Paris in 1651, was to have the greatest influence, particularly after it was 'English'd by J.G.D.' and appeared as *The French Cook* in London in 1653. It included recipes for hash, and for dishes both 'à la daube' and 'à la mode'. By 1688 cooks' glossaries included a wide range of newly introduced French terms, including:

A-la-Sauces Sauce made after the French Almaigne or German fashion.

A-la-Doode is a French way of ordering any large Fowl or Leg of Mutton.

A-la-Mode way is the new, or French way of dressing all manner of boiled or baked Meat.

Bouillon is a kind of Broth or boiled meat made of several things.

Hash is a Dishmeat made of any kind of flesh minced or in Gobbets stewed in strong broth with spices, and served up in a Dish with Sippets: to Hash is to stew any Meat that is cold. The French call it Hach or Hachee.

'We have said how necessary it is that in the composure of a sallet, every plant should come in to bear its part, without being overpower'd by some herb of a stronger taste, so as to endanger the native sapor and virtue of the rest; but fall into their places, like the notes in music, in which there should be nothing harsh or grating: And though admitting some discords (to distinguish and illustrate the rest) striking in all the more sprightly, and sometimes gentler notes, reconcile all dissonances, and melt them into an agreeable composition.'

John Evelyn, *Acetaria: a Discourse of Sallets,* 1699

Although a number of new dishes were introduced from other European countries – Italian dishes such as macaroni and vermicelli and Spain's olla podrida (a variety of stewed meats and vegetables, anglicised as 'hotch-potch') – the French influence was predominant. Even so, it did not overwhelm the native English taste for good, plain cooking. Many still preferred substantial, solid, wholesome roast and boiled meats to the highly priced Frenchified

Hogg-podg Dish-meats, neither pleasing to the Pallet, or of credit to the Masters … But let Cooks study new Dish-meats and work out their Brains, when they have done all they can, there are but four sorts of Meat which they can properly, and with safety, work upon, viz. Flesh of Beasts, Flesh of Fowle, Flesh of Fish and Field Fruits; and these again are according to their kinds either Stewed, Boiled, Parboiled, Fryed, Broiled, Roasted, Baked, Hashed, Pickled, Souced, or made into Sweet-Meats. Nil Ultra.

By the start of the 17th century, most modern foodstuffs had already been introduced. The parks and farms of the English countryside were producing venison and all other kinds of game, mutton, pork and beef, while an increasing quantity of beef was also being imported from Scotland. Ever since the Union of the Crowns in 1603, great herds of black cattle had been driven south over the border, slowly working their way down to London with beasts being sold off at fairs en route. On all but the poorest tables some three-quarters of every meal would consist of meat. Much of this was freshly killed but various techniques of salting and potting enabled it to be preserved for use throughout the winter months.

Most of the vegetables known today were also on the 17th-century menu. Common, or sweet, Virginian and Canadian potatoes were grown here too but they were still regarded as a novelty. The interest in gardening which had begun in the later 16th century continued to grow; orchards and gardens now yielded a wealth of fruit in addition to lettuce, chicory, celery, cucumbers and radishes. The earlier suspicion of raw vegetables and fruit was slowly subsiding and salads were appearing on the table with increasing frequency. In 1699 John Evelyn published a whole book on the subject, *Acetaria: a Discourse of Sallets*; in it he suggested a dressing made of three parts olive oil, one part vinegar, lemon or orange juice, dry mustard and mashed hard-boiled egg yolks.

New foodstuffs imported from overseas during this period included allspice or Jamaica pepper from the West Indies, cochineal from Mexico and sago from Malaya. From the 1640s, English colonists in Barbados turned their land over to sugar cane, so that sugar became plentiful and easily available leading to a great increase in the production of home-made preserves, confectionery and syrups. However, the most significant development was in the type of drinks enjoyed. By the 1660s it was possible to purchase in London: 'That excellent and by all Physitians approved China drink called by the Chineans Tcha, by other nations Tay alias Tee', 'Coffa, which is a blacke kind of drinke made of a kind of Pulse like Pease, called Coaus', which came from Arabia and Turkey, and chocolate, from the West Indies. Despite complaints that these novel drinks would damage the trade in home-grown barley and malt, in addition to making men 'as unfruitful as the deserts', they all enjoyed a popularity which has continued unabated to the present day.

A fashion plate of *c.*1695 showing a lady taking coffee.

'Would'st thou both eat thy cake and have it?'

George Herbert, English poet, 1593–1633

In addition to these new and exotic dishes, great strides were being made in the use of traditional home-grown produce. This was most clearly seen in bakery where a whole host of significant developments were taking place. The 'great cakes' of the medieval period continued to be popular for important occasions but now they were contained within a tinplate hoop, which made them much more convenient both to bake and to serve. One new variety was the Banbury cake; specially baked for wedding feasts, it had an outer layer of plain dough which concealed a rich filling of dough mixed with currants. It was in this period too that the modern baked gingerbread appeared, this somewhat sticky sponge flavoured with ginger and cinnamon replacing the earlier solid paste of highly spiced breadcrumbs.

Biscuits went through a similar transformation. The medieval biscuit had been made by dusting slices of an enriched bread roll with sugar and spices before returning them to the oven where they hardened into a kind of sweet rusk. Now, baked in the form of a single, light, finely-textured loaf, the biscuit-bread was often called 'fine cake' in contemporary recipe books. Other popular varieties of biscuit were 'gumballs' or 'jumbals', in which caraway-flavoured dough was worked up into knots or plaits, and Shrewsbury cakes, whose rounds of shortcake could be spiced with ginger or cinnamon.

As baking skills developed throughout England, some areas acquired a reputation for their own local specialities. This was particularly true of a number of northern towns, Chorley, Eccles, Dewsbury and Halifax giving their names to distinct variations of currant pastry.

Savoury black and white puddings forced into animal guts had been made for generations, but the early 17th century saw the development of that great English invention, the pudding cloth. Utilising this simple device it was possible to convert flour, milk, eggs, butter, sugar, suet, marrow and raisins into a whole series of hot, filling and nutritious dishes with minimal time, trouble and cost. With the ingredients securely tied within the cloth, the pudding had only to be plunged into a boiling pot, perhaps along with the meat and vegetables, where it could simmer for hours without further attention. Varying in texture and quality from light, moist custards to substantial masses of heavily fruited oatmeal, the boiled pudding soon became a mainstay of English cookery, being adopted by all sections of society.

Further puddings or 'pudding pies' were poured into dishes and baked in the oven. Rice puddings were readily made in this way, as were 'whitepots', the luxurious predecessors of bread-and-butter pudding.

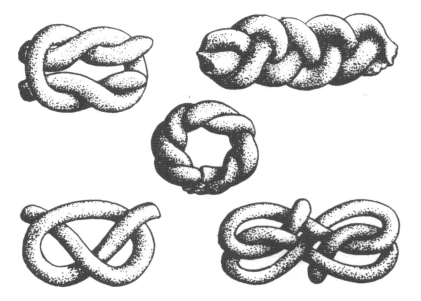

Designs for gumballs or jumbals

SUET PUDDING AND SMUGGLED TEA – EATING AND DRINKING IN THE GEORGIAN ERA

In 1700 the English still lived and ate in a way that would have seemed familiar to their medieval ancestors: agricultural, self-sufficient, killing cattle in winter, eating thick pottages. By 1800 England was on the brink of the modern era, seeing a widespread move off the land into the towns, the rise of a prosperous middle class, the development of newspapers and advertising and the birth of a consumer society.

Because of the increasing use of sugar, which made food more palatable, many of the old spices, flavourings and colourings, such as ambergris and musk, saffron and red sanders (sandalwood), went out of fashion, as did native pot-herbs such as daisies and violets. Raw green sauces and mashed herbs and vinegar were replaced by pickles, ketchups and, later in the century, bottled sauces.

Food also became simpler; for example, new sauces were developed tasting of one thing only: parsley or mustard or anchovy. But the universal sauce for vegetables was melted butter sauce invariably served in over-generous amounts. Thomas Turner, a Sussex shopkeeper, dining at his uncle's on 17 October 1756, had roasted pig and very good turnips, 'but spoiled by almost swimming in butter and also a butter pond pudding and

'Oh! The roast beef
of England. And old
England's roast beef.'

Henry Fielding, *Grub Street Opera III, 3*

that justly called, for there was almost but enough in it to have drowned the pig, had it been alive'. Butter, in spite of its expense, was used lavishly in almost every dish.

Advances in agriculture brought changes to the type of food available. At the beginning of the century cattle had to be killed at the start of winter because there was no fodder, so salt meat was eaten until the following spring or summer. Now winter feeding practices were copied from Dutch farmers and cattle could be kept through the winter. Enclosure of land and improved breeding with superior strains from Holland meant that the quality of meat improved dramatically, though this did not happen on a wide scale until the end of the century. Farm animals began to replace wild ones in the nation's diet, especially as game became more and more the prerogative of the landowner through enclosures and severe game laws.

Foreign visitors were amazed at English meat-eating. What M Misson said in the 1690s of the English (except for the poorer people) held true for the whole of the 18th century:

> *I always heard that they were great flesh-eaters, and I found it true. I have known people in England that never eat any bread, and universally they eat very little; they nibble a few crumbs, while they chew meat by whole mouthfuls... Among the middling sort of people they had 10 or 12 sorts of common meats which infallibly takes their turns at their tables, and two dishes are their dinners: a pudding, for instance, and a piece of roast beef.*

Habits in fish-eating changed too. Improved transport by the end of the century meant that sea fish could be carried to the towns in barrels of sea water comparatively quickly. As a result many freshwater fish, with their muddier taste, went out of favour with only the better species such as carp, pike and eel remaining popular. Fish ponds gradually became redundant and were turned into ornamental ponds. Oysters were plentiful and were still eaten in large numbers.

Pudding continued to be an English phenomenon. It took the place of cereal pottage as a starchy filler and by the 1740s roast beef and plum pudding had become a national dish. The increased use of the pudding cloth meant that pudding could be made at any time and the varieties proliferated so that foreign visitors were astonished. M Misson wrote:

> They bake them in the oven, they boil them with the meat, they make them 50 several ways: BLESSED BE HE THAT INVENTED PUDDING, for it is a manna that hits the palates of all sorts of people… [and they] are never weary of it.

Thomas Turner has as many as three puddings at once. On 15 November 1759 his dinner is 'a fine piece of beef roasted, a currant pond pudding, a currant suet pudding and a butter pudding cake' (all boiled).

The other filler, bread, was eaten sparingly by the well-off but it was eaten increasingly by the poor where it was their staple food. In the Midlands and the South white bread became available for the first time to the poor who then scorned rougher bread when bad harvests struck later in the 18th century. Cake was eaten at breakfast and afternoon tea. The traditional raising agent was wet ale yeast but eggs alone were soon found to be effective in raising a cake.

The wonderfully versatile suet pudding could be filled with beefsteak, giblets, pigeon, duck, raw fruit, currants and great ponds of butter. Boiled and baked puddings could be of rice, oatmeal, vermicelli, sago or custard. Sweet baked puddings, often cooked in a puff-pastry crust, were somewhat more elegant, and could be made with such things as curds, fruit, potatoes, carrots, spinach, custard, bread and butter, dried fruit and almonds.

The most common vegetables were cabbages, turnips and carrots, along with parsnips and onions. Potatoes were not eaten every day except in Ireland and parts of the North-West. Green vegetables, which had once been eaten in cereal pottages, were now simply boiled with melted butter sauce. Garden peas, French beans, asparagus, artichokes, cauliflower and celery were enjoyed by the well-off as were green salad items like lettuce and cucumber in summer. Tomatoes began to appear in recipes in the late 18th century but were not eaten raw until the end of the 19th.

Improved seed from Holland meant better varieties of vegetables and fruit appeared on English tables. Hothouses permitted the growing of grapes and peaches and even pineapples for the privileged. Raw fruit was at last acknowledged by medical opinion to be safe and now it was eaten as a healthy food. Garden rhubarb, introduced from Italy in the 17th century, was put into English tarts in the late 18th. Raw fruit was made into wine with the help of cheaper sugar. Fruit was bottled and made into jam, which was cheaper than butter as a spread for bread. Favourite fruits were damsons and gooseberries, and the favourite garnish was lemons.

Coffee, chocolate and tea had been introduced in the late 17th century. Chocolate was at first mixed with wine, then water. It came in a cake or roll and had to be grated into hot liquid, then swizzled with a notched stick called a chocolate mill (it was not made into chocolate bars until the end of the century). All three beverages were drunk sweetened as people were used to adding sugar to their wine. Coffee was drunk mainly by the well-to-do; it was expensive and could not be faked. Tea, from China, was so expensive that it would be kept in a locked caddy; it was

Opposite The rich enjoyed the luxury of pineapples which were grown in hothouses.
Below Damsons were one of the most popular fruits of the Georgian era.

Gambling was common and it was at the gaming table that the sandwich was invented. In 1760 John Montague, 4th Earl of Sandwich, called for his meat to be put between two pieces of bread so that he could carry on playing uninterrupted.

consequently made very weak, and drunk sweetened and without milk at first. However, both tea and coffee were recognised as stimulant drugs and milk began to be added to these drinks as it was believed that it would lessen the effect of the caffeine. Because of the high customs duties on tea, smuggling was carried out on a large scale. Parson Woodforde records in his diary, 29 March 1777:

Andrews the Smuggler brought me this night about 11 o'clock a bag of Hyson tea 6 pound weight. He frightened us a little by whistling under the parlour window just as we were going to bed. I gave him some Geneva and paid him for the tea 10s 6d per pound.

Ever-improving transport meant that regional specialities such as Scotch salmon, Newcastle salted haddock and Cheddar, Gloucester, Cheshire and Stilton cheeses came to be widely known. More reliable overseas transport brought foreign food such as sea turtles from the West Indies (those who could not afford it made mock turtle dishes); sago from Malaya; vermicelli, macaroni and Parmesan from Italy; piccalilli, punch, curry, rice and pickled mangoes from India; and ketchups from China and Malaya. Ketchups (the word comes from a Chinese word denoting brine from pickled fish or shellfish) were imitated, and bottled sauces were produced commercially at the end of the century, the first being Lazenby's anchovy essence and Harvey's sauce. Ready-mixed curry powder was on sale from the 1780s.

Butcher's meat was cheap but butter was double the price of meat. The prices recorded by the Revd. J Ismay in 1755 in Mirfield, West Yorkshire, are typical: beef, mutton and veal were 2d to 3d a pound, butter 5d to 6d and cheese 3d to 4d, while a roasting pig

SUBSTITUTES for BREAD ; — or — Right Honorables, Saving the Loaves: & Dividing the Fishe

Charitable Committee, for reducing the high price of Corn, by providing Substitutes for Bread in their own Families, this representation of t
hifts made by the Framers & Signers of the Philanthropic Agreement, is most respectfully dedicated.

Pub.d Dec.r 24.1795. by H.Humphrey New Bo

was 2s, a Christmas goose or turkey 2s 6d, a hen 7d and ducks 8d. In 1759 Thomas Turner paid 9s 3d for a pound of green tea, and in 1777 Parson Woodforde paid 10s 6d, though tea could fetch as much as 3 guineas a pound. A bottle of ordinary wine was 2s.

However, it was the fluctuating price of wheat which had the most effect on the poor. Comparing the prices with wages shows that working men could not afford to eat well: weavers earned only 5d a day, tailors only 6d plus food, farm labourers 7d, day labourers 1s, carpenters and masons 1s 3d. Shopkeepers, tradesmen and master craftsmen might get £1 a week and could afford to eat meat every day. Wages in London were higher but then so were prices.

Life for the poorer classes was a constant struggle. Many country labourers had lost their small homes and vegetable plots as a result of the 18th-century enclosing of land. They were reduced almost to paupers by having to buy food at exorbitant prices during the war with France. Yet peace brought them no relief. The farmers persuaded the government to keep the price of corn, and therefore bread, high. Wages did not rise but unemployment did and when bad harvests followed, there were widespread food riots. In desperation, thousands of men, with wives and children, trekked to the squalid slums of the growing cities to work in the newly established factories. A rural cottager who kept his job might still be able to afford a bit of bacon on Sundays, though on other days his family lived largely on bread with a little flavoured lard and potatoes. In the cities, bread and potatoes or porridge were almost the only foods of slum-dwellers. Strong tea, giving an illusion of warmth and fullness, was the main comfort of both urban and rural poor.

Substitutes for Bread, or Right Honourables Saving the Loaves & Dividing the Fishes, 1795, by James Gillray: Georgian political caricature showing the Prime Minister William Pitt and his cabinet feasting during a food shortage crisis.

'I am not without hopes of tempting Mrs. Lloyd to settle in Bath; meat is only 8*d.* per pound, butter 12*d.*, and cheese 9½ *d.* You must carefully conceal from her, however, the exorbitant price of fish: a salmon has been sold at 2*s.* 9*d.* per pound the whole fish. The Duchess of York's removal is expected to make that article more reasonable – and till it really appears so, say nothing about salmon.'

Letter written by Jane Austen to her sister Cassandra, 5 May 1801

Descriptions of Jane Austen's home life provide a good idea of what middle-class people ate by the end of the 18th century. Her father was a modest country clergyman, fairly typical of his class. He farmed enough land to grow wheat for home bread-making and kept cows, pigs and sheep for mutton, a favourite standard joint. Lamb at that time meant baby lamb, a delicate dinner-party meat. Mrs Austen kept poultry. The only foods she had to buy were game, fish and imported goods such as tea, coffee and sugar. She had a vegetable garden and fruit trees, and taught her daughters to supervise their maids in making butter, cheese, preserves, pickles and homemade wines, and in brewing beer and curing bacons and hams. When they moved into the town, prices loomed much larger in the family's thinking and the cost of meat especially seemed frighteningly high. But they still ate well, if more simply than their grand neighbours.

Some members of the aristocracy still found it important to display their wealth and power on a massive scale, one instance being the Earl of Warwick's outdoor banquet for 6,000 in 1746, described by Horace Walpole. The court was not so ostentatious. In view of the patriotism attached to the roast beef of old England it is not surprising to discover that the king and his court at St James's Palace, when not entertaining, ate rather plain food. In 1740, when Paris was getting nouvelle cuisine, George II and his household were eating good plain English fare though a few French names for dishes were thrown in for effect.

A gentleman now had for breakfast – instead of ale and cereal pottage – tea, coffee or chocolate (the last going out of fashion as the century advanced), and 'whigs' (rich bread rolls), buttered toast or cake. Sometimes he had broth or water gruel.

Supper was taken by those who had dined at midday. It usually consisted, at least among the tradesman class, of cold meats, cold pies and tarts. A typical company supper in February 1758, enjoyed with his neighbours by Thomas Turner, consisted of cold roast beef, cold roast goose, cold tongue, cold apple pasty, bread and cheese. After these suppers, Turner and his wife usually played at cards, winning or losing as much as five shillings, and drank into the early hours of the morning. He was frequently drunk and his over-indulgence typifies the widespread drunkenness which affected all classes in the 18th century.

Strong drink was cheap and widely available. Because of the troubles with France which started in the late 17th century, French wines and brandy became scarce and expensive (and widely smuggled), and Portuguese and Spanish wines were drunk instead. In the hope of reducing smuggling, the government encouraged the production of home-made wines and brandy. This was so successful, and spirits were so cheap, that scenes such as that depicted by William Hogarth in his series of engravings *Gin Lane* were common, with the gin shop notice declaring 'drunk for a penny, dead drunk for two-pence, clean straw for nothing'. In Scotland even the poor drank neat whisky with their meals.

In all classes drunkenness and gambling went together, along with rough or cruel sports typifying a callousness which was reflected in the cruel treatment of creatures intended for food. Living fish were slashed to make the flesh contract (known as 'crimping'); eels were skinned alive; lobsters roasted alive; turkeys were suspended by the feet and bled to death from the mouth; bulls were baited before slaughter to make the meat more tender and pigs and calves were lashed for the same reason.

Gin drinking during the 18th century, particularly among the poorer classes, became a craze. Known as Geneva from the French word for juniper, *genièvre*, it was cheap and widely available. In 1730 over six and a half million gallons of 'official' gin a year were consumed, on top of the quantities of illegal, often dangerously adulterated, gin bought from illicit suppliers, and by 1750 the annual total was over eleven million gallons. In 1751 over 9,000 children died after being given gin to keep them quiet.

Gin Lane by William Hogarth, 1751.

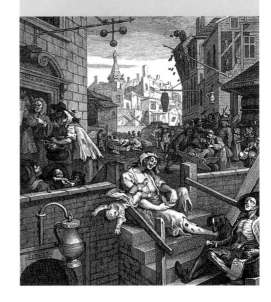

One of William Kitchiner's recipes begins, 'Take a red cock that is not too old and beat him to death.' Towards the end of the century a growing sensibility caused increasing revulsion against these cruelties.

This century of unbridled appetite took its toll on the nation's health. Such massive amounts of protein, animal fat and alcohol, in the absence of fibrous vegetables or coarse bread, coupled with a sedentary existence and smoking, caused problems. The high proportion of salt meat eaten in Scotland contributed to the rise in cases of heart disease there. Gout, diabetes and cirrhosis of the liver were common and deficiency diseases such as scurvy and rickets increased towards the end of the century, especially in towns. In Wales and the North where the staple diet included larger amounts of barley or oats, the population was healthier. The labouring classes in the Midlands and the South, however, fared badly. They lived on bought bread and cheese enlivened with a few potatoes and washed down with tea, which by the end of the century had become a necessity to them to replace the now expensive beer that had once supplied them with both calories and vitamins

Hydros and spas became fashionable in an effort to improve health. However, at Bath in Somerset, where people flocked to take the waters during the day, most spoiled any benefits they gained by debauching themselves in the gay social whirl of dinners, balls and theatres at night.

Simple porridge made from oats was a staple of the North of England and Wales.

THE VICTORIAN LARDER – POVERTY AND PLENTY IN THE AGE OF INDUSTRIALISATION

Queen Victoria reigned for more than 60 years after succeeding to the throne in 1837 at the age of 18. Her life, spanning most of the 19th century, saw enormous developments both politically and socially. It was an era in which great changes were made to the way in which food was prepared and eaten and in the variety available.

By the early 19th century things had gone from bad to worse for the poorer classes. In contrast, the middle classes, especially the growing numbers in the cities, were prospering. The new cheap labour pool there was helping to create an industrial and commercial boom – in new food industries among others. The development of macadamised roads and long-distance railways made it possible to transport factory-made and processed goods in bulk quickly and easily. The gap between even the modestly well paid and the workers widened.

By 1845 the situation was desperate. The poor corn harvest and the falling wage levels added to the misery of the poor. The potato fungus brought famine and starvation to Ireland and to parts of Scotland and England where potatoes now were the main or only food of the poor. The government was forced, at last, to bring down the price of bread.

'The rule is jam tomorrow and jam yesterday, but never jam today.'

Lewis Carroll
(Charles Lutwidge Dodgson), 1819–80

The famine also brought home to some of the better-off how many of the working people they called 'the poor' were actually destitute, and made them want to do something for the starving. For instance, two renowned London chefs, Alexis Soyer and Charles Francatelli, more used to handling delicacies such as ortolans (small birds) and truffles, designed new soup recipes to provide cheap food for the masses. The soups had little nourishment but the gesture marked the start of a new humanitarian movement.

After 1848 the variety, quality and freshness of food in the cities began to improve for everyone, mainly because the railways distributed fresh foods, such as milk, and the new, bulk-processed foods efficiently and quickly. The urban middle classes benefited most. They were becoming more and more prosperous and conscious of their rising social status. They ate well to show it off and, since they did not grow or preserve their own food, they bought the new, better-quality meat and vegetables and the mass-produced and mass-preserved foods which now came into the shops.

Poor people also began to eat slightly better. By 1864 a country labourer with a job could afford one hot meal a week and some vegetables. Better-off artisans might have a cheap knuckle joint now and then, cooked at the baker's, or get a midday meal of meat and root vegetables, bread, cheese and beer at a tavern or basement cookshop (a shop where cooked food was sold).

Even the poor, who still subsisted mostly on bread and potatoes, were catered for by manufacturers and importers of the cheapest new mass-market foods. For instance, when cattle disease sent meat prices sky-high in 1865, importers bought in cheap, fatty American bacon and Australian canned meats. Poor folk could also now get cheap, dark treacle to flavour their bread. Then, towards the end of the 19th century, cheap jam made of coloured, sweetened vegetables or fruit pulp offered them a sweeter, if less nourishing, alternative.

The poor benefited from another development. In 1861 roller mills came into use in Britain, by the 1870s giving everyone refined white flour without wheatgerm. However, most of the new processed packeted, bottled and canned foods which came in during the second half of the 19th century were only for people who lived 'above stairs'. The poor could neither afford them nor make use of them.

The following are a few of the processed foods which changed the look and taste of the dishes on middle-class tables:

◆ Quick-acting compressed yeast, self-raising flour, and baking powder – these significantly changed bread and cake-making recipes.
◆ Custard powder, blancmange powder and concentrated egg powder.
◆ Bottled, gelatine-based jellies and, later, stiffer table jellies in packets. These let housewives with little time and money make elaborate desserts like those of the wealthy.
◆ Bulk-produced cheese made in factories. This replaced farm cheese.
◆ Sweetened condensed milk and dried milk.
◆ Margarine (at first made from beef and milk). It was cheap, although it tasted oily and insipid to begin with.
◆ Bulk-dried vegetables and dried packeted soups.
◆ Commercially bottled pickles and sauces. Some, such as the products of Harry J Heinz, had a novelty value at first but soon became household names.

Advertisement for Heinz pickles, *c*.1900.

Experiments in bottling and canning meat in bulk had been going on since the beginning of the 19th century in both France and England, not to help the housewife but to feed the troops and sailors. In 1865 the Admiralty set up the first large-scale meat-canning factory and ten years later canned meats from both Australia and America were being imported. This marked a significant change – by the end of the 19th century Britain had come to depend on imported food.

Fish supplies to the expanding cities before the 1850s had been insufficient and more than often rotten or tainted. The supply improved rapidly when steam trawlers replaced the old sailing boats and the invention of trawling made cod an everyday fish instead of a luxury one. As the railways spread and trains became faster, fish even reached inland towns safely, packed in ice imported in bulk from Iceland and Norway. The ice-man who brought a great dripping block of ice to a well-to-do Victorian home before a dinner party became a familiar sight. However, another familiar sight now disappeared: due to over-fishing and pollution the oysters, which had been a staple food for the very poor and common since prehistoric times, became an almost unobtainable luxury and oyster stalls in the poor quarters of London began to close down from around 1850.

Illustration by Thomas Crane in *London Town*, *c*.1880.

The Penny-Ice Man

IN summer when the sun is high,
    And children's lips are parched and dry,
An ice is just the thing to try.
So this young man who comes, 'tis plain,
    From Saffron Hill or Leather Lane,
A store of pence will quickly gain.
"A lemon ice for me," says Fred ;
    Cries Sue, "No, have a cream instead."
"A raspberry !" shouts Newsboy Ned.
"What fun ! Although we're now in June,
    It feels"—says Ned—"this afternoon,
Like eating winter with a spoon !"

Chilling or freezing meat in bulk was not practical until a cheap way of making ice was found in 1861. Even then, it took until 1880 to find a way of refrigerating and transporting bulk meat in good condition; so chilled and frozen meat became a major source of supply only at the end of the century.

By the end of the Victorian era, the cook's store cupboard in the middle-class city home was as full of packets and cans as any modern kitchen. With the help of bottled sauces, canned vegetables and fruit, and essences, the cook could choose between as many flavours (if less subtle ones) as a skilled chef who still made all his kitchen 'basics' by hand. Most fresh foods came to her door. The baker and muffin-man called daily. The fishmonger with his ice-laden cart brought cod, hake, salmon, skate, eels, herrings and shellfish; even lobsters were still a reasonable price. The cook could buy most vegetables in season from the greengrocer's cart, from asparagus in spring to pumpkin at Hallowe'en, though she would have to prepare all her vegetables and her fish herself. Her milkman would still fill her jug with milk or cream from his churn; bottling and pasteurisation did not come in until the 1920s, although from the 1860s railway transport from the country, machine milking and cooking gave her cleaner milk.

She would really only have to leave her basement kitchen to visit the butcher and poulterer. Veal was still the cheapest meat to use for everyday meals and white stock; the family would not despise a well-dressed calf's head and the feet still reputedly made the best jelly. Mutton had gone down a little in the social scale; Irish stew was now made from scrag and was a servants' dish, though a roasted joint looked handsome on the dinner table. A

'It is not worth the while to live by rich cookery.'

Henry David Thoreau, 1817–62

fine chicken or capon was as much a party dish as was a pheasant and small birds such as woodcock and snipe made popular savouries.

Among the working class some poorer slum children still had only porridge or bread and jam for the majority of their meals in the week, and there were many waifs who got less. But there was a strong humanitarian movement now to help the needy. Well-meaning people produced dozens of cookbooks aimed at helping the poor – although these were not as a rule very practical because few ordinary people knew anything about nutrition yet, or the real problems faced by the needy.

In rural areas conditions and wages varied. In some places labourers and their families did not get enough to eat and suffered greatly. However, many farmers gave their workers food perks or paid them with food in exchange for overtime, and most still let women and children into the fields to glean after the harvest. Children got off school to go nutting in season or to pick field mushrooms.

By the end of the Victorian era there were many grades of working people. At the lowest end of the social scale diets were very restricted but some working people, such as skilled craftsmen or the upper servants in a big house, now lived almost as well as their employers.

Culinary organisation –
techniques, equipment and tools

ROMAN SOPHISTICATION AND SPECIALISATION

The complex recipes of Roman Britain required more careful cooking than the simple stews, roasts and pottages of the preceding prehistoric cooking tradition, and it is therefore not surprising to find that the Romans used more sophisticated equipment. Roman cooking was usually done over a charcoal fire on a raised brick hearth, with cooking vessels resting on tripods or gridirons; meat and fish could be directly grilled over burning charcoal on the gridiron. It is possible that wood was burnt on the raised hearths too, especially in the case of dishes which Apicius describes as being smoked. Some very ornamental water heaters were discovered at Pompeii which may have been used for keeping food warm, or possibly for cooking by the bain-marie method of putting the cooking vessels in a dish of boiling water. For boiling sucking pig in a cauldron it was likely, in country kitchens at any rate, that the pig was suspended by chains from the rafters over a more conventional open fire. Wild boar and other large animals were also roasted on spits over wood fires.

Ovens were used for baking and roasting. They were constructed of rubble and tiles, shaped like low beehives with a flue to give a draught. Wood or charcoal fires were then lit inside them and, as soon as the required temperature was reached, the ashes were raked out and the food was put in. The opening of the oven was then covered to retain the heat. There were also a range of *clibanus,* portable ovens made of earthenware or iron that were used for baking bread or keeping dishes warm. They seem to have had double walls with a rounded vault wider at the base than at the top. A charcoal fire must have been made under the inner floor so that the heat could percolate between the walls with the fumes escaping through small holes in the outer wall. These ovens were suitable for cooking roast neck of mutton, sucking kid or lamb, kidneys and stuffed dormice.

Built ovens have been recorded from a number of different sites: at Cirencester a row of 4th-century shops were all equipped with ovens and may have been bakeries. They are a feature on many villa sites and good examples occur at Great Witcombe and Chedworth in Gloucestershire. They have also been found on military sites, sometimes backing on to the ramparts as at Carleon.

Meat was cooked by roasting over a low fire on a gridiron or in a portable oven but particularly large joints were either cooked in a baker's oven or grilled on spits over an open fire. Meat was also stewed in an iron cauldron suspended over an open hearth. Metal cooking pots became increasingly popular as clay vessels were porous and almost impossible to clean effectively. Mass production of small metal cauldrons meant that they became so cheap they could be thrown away when they became unfit for use. In contrast, bronze cookery equipment was more costly and would have been repaired rather than discarded. A hoard of bronze cooking vessels and a gridiron were found at the legionary fortress at Newstead, Yorkshire, and some had been repaired using soldered bronze patches.

The Romans had a sophisticated array of specialised cooking pans. The frying pan (*fretale* or *sartago*) was sometimes

A Roman mosaic of a baker using a beehive oven.

equipped with a folding handle so that it could be put inside the portable oven, as well as being used for cooking over the gridiron. The *patella* was a round shallow pan with a handle, a little deeper than the frying pan, which was used on the table as well as in the kitchen. The *patina* appears to have been an even deeper vessel rather like a casserole without a lid and this was used for making complex dishes with a number of ingredients.

Two other vessels which featured in the Roman kitchen were *mortaria* and *amphorae*. Mortaria were used as general-purpose mixing bowls and had roughened inner surfaces, heavy rims for lifting and a spout for pouring. They were first introduced by the Roman army but local potteries soon began to make them. A number of huge mortaria, perhaps for use in bakeries, were made in Germany in the 2nd century and imported into Britain.

Amphorae were used in large quantities by the Romans for transporting and storing wine and oil and remains of hundreds of them have been found in Britain. After serving their primary purpose, they were often adapted for other uses – set in the floor to store water or even used as coffins. They varied in design from the early carrot-shaped type with small handles to more elegant versions with long necks, elongated handles and pointed bases, and globular forms with short necks and smaller handles. In general it seems that the tall amphorae came from France and contained wine while the globular amphorae came from Spain, full of precious olive oil.

MEDIEVAL SPURTLES AND PANSHONS

A wide variety of cooking methods were practised in the Middle Ages depending on the size and wealth of the household and the facilities available. A rural cottager, whether free, tenant or serf, had only a one-room home with a fire built on a large flat stone in the centre or against a wall if the hut had stone walls. If a beam stretched across the hut, the housewife might have a cast-iron cauldron hanging from it – but she was more likely to use earthenware pots standing in the hot ashes beside the fire, or balanced on a tall stone among the embers. She could 'seethe', or boil, her pottage in this way, stirring it with a ladle or 'spurtle' (a wooden stick). Small birds, hedgehogs or a squirrel might be wrapped in clay and baked in the hottest ashes, as might fresh fish, but salt herring was best boiled.

If she wanted to bake, she needed more equipment. Although the manorial lord demanded that his peasants should get their corn ground by his licensed miller for a fee, it was hard for him to enforce this and many people ground their small quantity of grain in a hardwood mortar, a stone trough or a hand-quern. They then mixed it with water and baked unleavened bread or oatcakes on the hearth under an upturned pot.

A village tradesman or artisan lived almost as simply, but his home would probably have had two rooms with the fire in the living area. There might be iron firedogs on either side of the

hearth to support an iron rod from which a cauldron could be hung. A poor housewife would be lucky to have a couple of pottery or wooden bowls to make cream or cheese in, and she would probably have churned her butter by hand, but her grander neighbour who kept a cow might well have had a new-style plunger churn worked like a pestle and mortar with a lid.

A castle, manor house or monastery would have a whole complex of rooms to prepare and store food with a kitchen, larders, storerooms, cellars, a buttery where drink was stored and a pantry from where bread, trenchers and salt were served. The kitchen was generally stone-floored and walled with a great wide fireplace where most of the cooking was done. Meat was roasted on spits over the fire but sometimes, especially if very large joints required cooking, this took place in a separate building to reduce the risk of fire. In 1206 King John had separate kitchens built at Clarendon, each of which had fires which could roast two or three whole oxen.

Simple roasting spits were propped on firedogs and turned by apprentice cooks or kitchen-boys. There were no women cooks or kitchen maids yet. Boy scullions cleaned the spits and ladles, as well as the bowls and brushes used for applying egg-wash to add a sheen to the near-roasted joints. The kitchen was where they worked and slept and they were rarely allowed into the other rooms of the kitchen complex.

The bakehouse was usually a separate building with ovens built against the walls. Bread, pies and

A pair of kitchen boys turn a roasting spit in a medieval kitchen.

pastries were baked in much the same way as they had been during the Roman period with the oven being heated to the required temperature first by burning wood, peat or gorse. The dairy was another separate structure where shallow 'panshons', wide earthern vessels, were kept to hold the milk. A heavy cheese-press would stand in one corner and ladles, skimmers, jugs and brushes would be hung on the walls.

The professional medieval cook had two other cooking appliances: one was a grid of metal bars on a long handle which was used to broil food over the fire, instead of under it as with a modern grill. The other resembled a two-sided waffle-iron and was used to make crisp batter wafers.

The cook had, of course, other kitchen tools: cleavers, knives and mallets, special tongs for cutting sugar, bunches of twigs for whisking and scouring, pestles and mortars of all sizes and weights, to name just a few. Plus cloths, scouring sand and tubs so the scullions could do the washing up!

The kitchen fireplace in the keep of Carlisle Castle, Cumbria.

ROYAL INFLUENCE IN TUDOR COOKERY

As in most aspects of fashionable Tudor life, the sovereign and the courtiers set the required standards of taste in all aspects of cookery and eating habits. At the court itself, based in one of the massive palaces at Whitehall, Richmond, Hampton Court, Nonsuch or Greenwich, vast quantities of high-quality food had to be prepared for perhaps 1,500 or more diners every day. Each establishment therefore had a vast series of domestic buildings, including cellars, pantries, bakehouses and kitchens lined with wide-arched fireplaces that could cope with cooking the large quantities of meat eaten when the court was in residence.

Similar facilities, albeit on a smaller scale, were demanded by the great landowning families in their magnificent new houses. Mansions such as Burghley and Longleat incorporated excellent catering facilities capable of dealing with the family's everyday requirements and the enormous demands occasioned by the annual visits of the court during its progression through the country. In these houses, the overall domestic management was usually the responsibility of the steward. The actual control of the kitchens, provisions and kitchen staff was then delegated to a clerk in the kitchen. The full extent of this officer's responsibilities, and the complex workings of a great Tudor establishment, are well illustrated in the *Booke of the Household of Queene Elizabeth* of 1600.

SINE SOLE
IRIS

'Good bread and good
   drink,
A good fire in the hall,
Brawn, pudding and souse,
And good mustard withal.
Beef, mutton and pork,
And good pies of the best,
Pig, veal, goose and capon,
And turkey well drest,
Cheese, apples and nuts,
And good carols to hear,
As then in the country
Is counted good cheer.'

Thomas Tusser,
500 Points of Husbandry, 1573

Working under the direction of the Lord Chamberlain, the Clerk to the Kitchen during the reign of Queen Elizabeth I controlled a total staff of 160, his 11 chief officers, either serjeants, chief clerks or master cooks, each representing specialist departments. For example, the Serjeant of the Accatry (the word is related to the verb 'to cater'), was responsible for obtaining beef and mutton from the queen's pastures, together with veal, pork, lard, sea fish, freshwater fish and salt. These were all passed to the Serjeant of the Larder whose Yeoman of the Boyling House boiled them as required. It is probable that the actual boilers were large permanent vessels of copper or brass set within masonry structures and heated by means of their own fireplaces and flues. Smaller quantities of meat would be boiled in metal cauldrons hung from a bar fixed across the chimney in a normal fireplace. Poultry, game birds and lambs were the responsibility of the Serjeant of the Poultry whose Yeoman of the Scalding House scalded, plucked and drew them ready for the cooks. Meanwhile, the Serjeant of the Bakehouse had a Yeoman Garnetor to maintain supplies of corn and flour, Yeoman Pervayers to carry supplies into the bakehouses and further yeomen and grooms who baked bread for both the queen's table and the entire household.

After the grain was measured and milled, the flour was 'boulted', or sieved, to remove the bran by shaking a quantity of flour through a piece of coarse canvas or linen, probably from Doulas in Brittany. In William Shakespeare's *Henry IV, Part I,* Falstaff gave away 'dowlas' to bakers' wives for them to use for 'boulters'. The fine flour was then kneaded with salt, yeast and water in a long wooden dough trough. After being worked into loaves and carefully weighed, the dough was next pricked or marked, allowed to rise, and slipped into the oven by means of a long oven-slice or 'peel'. The oven itself was still the beehive variety known since Roman times and used in the same way for baking. The oven doors were sealed closed with mud and the bread cooked in the heat retained by the masonry. When the bread was ready, the door had be smashed open. Similar ovens were used by the Serjeant of the Pastry who prepared all the baked meats, pastries and pies, ensuring that they were 'well seasoned with that proportion of spice which is allowed them, and well-filled, and made according to the rate which is appointed unto them… and see that no waste be made of sauces'. Meanwhile in the Spicery, the department of the household concerned with the keeping and mixing of spices, the Chief Clarke controlled the finer aspects of bakery, with yeomen to beat the spice into powder with pestles and mortars, yeomen to make wafers for festivals with beautifully decorated iron wafer-tongs, and further yeomen to run the Confectionary – the department which supplied pears, figs, raisins and other fruit.

The provision of all the equipment used throughout the royal kitchens was the responsibility of the Serjeant of the Scullery. As well as issuing 'chistes, guarde or irons, tubbes, trayes, baskets, flaskets [long shallow baskets], scoopes, broaches [spits], peeles and such like', he had full charge of all the silver and pewter dishes and candlesticks used on the royal tables.

The 16th-century *Ordinance of the Bakers of York* depicting different stages in the making of bread.

By combining these facilities with those of their own kitchens, the master cooks for the queen and her household were admirably equipped to prepare the elaborate dishes required by the court. As well as the usual range of utensils – knives, spoons, whisks, bowls and colanders – the master cook's most useful resource was probably the stove. This was a long masonry bench with a number of round firebaskets lined with sheet iron set into it. Fuelled with charcoal, the stove could be used just like one of today's gas or electric stoves, allowing small quantities of food to be heated either fiercely or gently, perhaps in a saucepan or a frying pan, while being stirred or beaten by the cook.

The preparation of fine food was by no means restricted to the professional cooks employed in the great households. The knowledge of the court cooks, exclusively male throughout the Middle Ages, was by Tudor times passing into the hands of the English gentlewomen who were to develop it to an outstanding degree over the coming centuries.

The kitchen at Portland Castle in Dorset which has been furnished in Tudor style.

STUART BROACHES AND KITCHEN DOGS

Cookery in the Stuart period continued to centre round large, broad-arched fireplaces where coal or log fires provided all the heat necessary for boiling and roasting. Boiling food in brass or iron cauldrons over the fire was one of the most economical ways of cooking and whole meals could be produced in a single operation. Joints of meat were plunged into the boiling water along with vegetables contained in net bags, as well as puddings which were tied up in cloths or floated in wooden bowls. Another way of boiling meat, particularly suitable for poultry and game, was to place the meat in an earthenware vessel along with some butter and herbs, seal the container with a lid held in place with a pastry strip and then immerse it in the cauldron for a few hours. In this way, richly flavoured and tender dishes such as jugged hare were produced.

A cast bronze skillet of 1684.

For roasting, meat was mounted on long iron spits or 'broaches' supported on spit dogs or 'cob-irons' and cooked in front of the fire. Turning the spit was still being done by hand – a long, boring and uncomfortable job as the turnspit would have his front roasted by the heat of the fire while his back was chilled by the cold draughts which rushed forward to fan the flames. It is not surprising that this was the first domestic process to be fully mechanised. From the early 17th century, weight-driven clockwork jacks mounted on the sides of the fireplaces began to be used to

'There is comprehended, under the curs of the coarsest kind, a certain dog in kitchen service excellent. For when any meat is to be roasted, they go into a wheel, which they turning about but with the weight of their bodies, so diligently look to their business, that no drudge or scullion can do the meat more cunningly, whom the popular sort hereupon term turnspits.'

Doctor Caius,
Founder of Caius College, Cambridge

turn the spits at a slow and uniform rate. However, in some kitchens dog-power was preferred. A wooden wheel with treads was attached to the spit and then a small dog was put inside and encouraged to keep running to turn the wheel.

Turning the meat was only one of the tasks involved in roasting. Before being secured on to the spit, game and poultry had to be cleaned and trussed while sucking pigs required more detailed attention. This most succulent of roasts had its mouth wedged open first before rigor mortis set in and was then stuffed with bread and herbs before being sewn up and mounted on the spit. Fat from the roasting pig was caught in a long, shallow dripping pan with a sloping base and then used to baste the meat to keep it moist and tender.

Saucepans made of iron, bronze, tinned copper or silver were used for heating smaller quantities of food. As they were difficult to use over the open fires, they were supported either on a 'brigg', a horizontal framework bridging the topmost firebars, or on a trivet, a tall three-legged iron stand which stood in front of the fire to take advantage of the radiant heat. Alternatively, a shorter version of the trivet, called a 'brandreth', could hold a pan just above the gentle heat of a small fire burning on the hearth. Skillets and 'posnets' were also used in this position, their pan-like bodies being raised on three integral legs.

In large establishments, where entertainment was provided on a lavish scale, the kitchen usually had a stove as well as the normal fireplace. This was a development of the long masonry bench used during the Tudor period which had several inset fire-baskets. Once filled with glowing charcoal, the stove provided a clean and easily controlled heat, ideal for delicate cooking and making sauces and preserves.

The only other cooking facility to be found in the Stuart kitchen was the beehive oven, which continued to survive into the 17th century. The way it was used had altered very little over the centuries and its main function was baking bread – one of the major tasks of any household. At the right time the mud which sealed the door was broken, the oven opened and the bread drawn out on a peel. As there was still a considerable quantity of heat left in the oven, puddings, pasties and pies which required longer, low-temperature cooking were then inserted. The door was sealed in place once again and the contents left to cook as long as necessary. The popularity of the beehive oven continued until the mid-18th century when the introduction of the first iron ovens proved to be an instant success because of their ability to provide a constant source of heat.

A London bakehouse, where the baker uses a long wooden peel to place the bread in a beehive oven.

NEW TECHNOLOGY IN THE GEORGIAN KITCHEN

Though cooking over an open fire continued to be popular, by about 1700 the 'range' or 'grate' – an iron fire-basket inside the hearth – became increasingly popular. The usual form of grate was a large oblong basket on four legs which was fastened to the chimney-back with tie bars. The spits were now usually turned mechanically by a clockwork spitjack and later by a smokejack inside the chimney which was operated by the heat of the fire. The fire could be made smaller by winding adjustable sides or 'cheeks' inwards by a rack-and-pinion mechanism while supports for pans could swing out over the fire. By the middle of the century, in fashionable town houses, panels of cast iron were added on each side with flat, iron plates on top to provide hobs.

The charcoal stove which had developed since the Tudor period continued to be used in the 18th century as it provided the gentle heat needed for delicate dishes. It was also far more comfortable for the cook who did not have to bend down to the hearth, though fumes were more of a problem. As late as 1800, James Woodforde recorded in his diary on 22 July that when his niece Nancy was making jam, 'she became giddy, too long at the stove where charcoal was burning, though the outward door was open all the time'.

The development in mid-century of the 'perpetual oven' was of enormous benefit. These were iron ovens with a grate

The kitchen of William Wordsworth's house in Cockermouth, Cumbria.

underneath and one of the earliest recorded was installed in 1750 at Shibden Hall, Halifax, for the Revd John Lister. However, only the wealthy could afford these expensive new cooking ovens – Lister had to pay over four guineas for his. Since the perpetual oven was often sited near the fireplace so that it could share the flue and chimney, it was a short step to combine oven and main fire. By 1770 in the north of England one of the iron panels at the side of the grate had been replaced by an iron oven heated from the side of the fire. This arrangement, known as a 'Yorkshire' range, had one major problem – it cooked unevenly – so a more expensive type was developed with flues running all round the oven and up the chimney. Later the grate's other iron panel was replaced by a water boiler which was filled and emptied through a hole in the hob top, and soon a tap was fitted for even more convenience.

As the fire was still open, however, a great deal of heat was lost up the chimney. This was solved by covering the fire with a further iron plate so that all the smoke was drawn through the

Kitchen and scullery plans (bottom) and elevation (above) of the 1780s, Bretton Hall, West Yorkshire. The new boiler at the back of the range was to supply kitchen and scullery with hot water and steam for the warm closet and steam table, both of iron (extreme right:. the pipe passes over the oven). It also supplied steam for the three kettles with taps (C) in the scullery. A is a double boiler with cast front and hob. B is a cast hot plate. The old oven and range were to be left intact. Note the new smokejack in the chimney.

Scullery   *Kitchen*

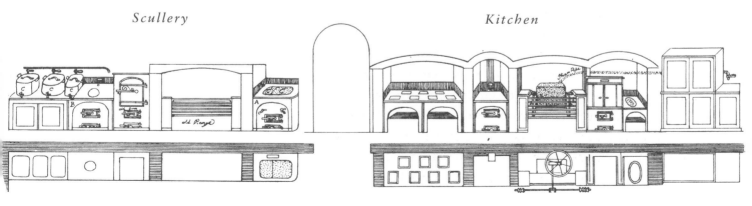

flues and up the chimney. The first patent for such a closed range was taken out in February 1802 by George Bodley, a Devonshire iron founder. His 'Kitchener' range was similar to the Yorkshire range, but it had a cast-iron hotplate over the fire with removable boiling rings. The new plate also provided a useful simmering hob – and made the old charcoal oven redundant. The front of the Kitchener range could also be enclosed by movable panels or a door to redirect the heat for boiling or baking instead of roasting. In the metal oven, with its polished tin interior to reflect the heat, it was now possible to roast the meat and bake a batter pudding at the same time. Thomas Turner records that on Christmas day 1756 they had 'a sirloin of beef roasted in the oven with a batter pudding under it'.

Poorer households could not afford an oven or even a spit and irons for roasting meat. The poor man's spit was nothing but a hook on a piece of string from which the piece of meat spun before the fire. This 'danglespit' was superseded by the clockwork bottlejack with a cast-iron balance wheel with four hooks to spit small birds or pieces of meat.

The majority of English people preferred plain food – roasted and boiled meat along with puddings and pies – and so large varieties of kitchen utensils were unnecessary. The rich and fashionable, however, often employed French cooks to make French dishes and these required a more extensive *batterie de cuisine*. William Verral, who worked for M de Clouet, the chef of the Duke of Newcastle, wrote an entertaining cookery book entitled A *Complete System of Cookery*, 1759. He lists the utensils which every kitchen of the well-to-do should have:

William Verral gives an amusing account of going to cook at a house in Sussex where the old gentleman typified many English people by wanting his meat plain, roast or boiled, and very little else. Although he was quite well off, his kitchen had little except one frying pan and one sieve – and that had been used for sanding the floor.

There were many hazards in the Georgian kitchen. Apart from the ever-present danger from fire, scalding and fumes, there were perils in the utensils themselves. Brass and copper pans, if used with acid food, could create poisonous verdigris. 'A whole family died', writes Hannah Glasse, 'owing to verdigrease' but even so, some fruits and pickles were deliberately cooked in these vessels in order to achieve a bright green colour. Alum and boiling vinegar were used to make apples green although too much could upset the stomach. Peach-laurel leaves were used to impart a bitter almond flavour which was only safe if the food was brought to a boil. Used tea-leaves were sold by servants to dealers who re-coloured them, often with poisonous materials, and then sold them on.

Stoves; 2 boilers, one to hold a leg of mutton, the other two fowls; A Soup-pot; Eight small Stew-pans, of different sizes, and their covers; Two very large [Stew-pans], and covers; A neat Frying-Pan; Two copper Ladles, tinned; 3 large copper Spoons, tinned; 2 Slices, tinned; An Egg-Spoon, tinned; A Pewter Cullendar; 4 Sieves – one of Lawn; 5 Copper-cups, to hold above 1/4 of a Pint; 6 Do. Smaller; 2 Etamines [for straining thick soup]; 3 large wooden Spoons; Sauce-Pans, Several.

Among other utensils he could have mentioned are: rolling pins, baking pins, cake hoops or tins, earthenware pans, bowls, knives, forks, graters, coffee mills, pestles and mortars, whisks, fritters, cabbage nets, pastry brush and jagging iron (an instrument used for ornamenting pastry, now made in the form of a toothed wheel set on a handle), skimmer, salamander, fish kettle, lemon squeezer, writing paper, pudding cloths, weighing scales, spice and peppermills, patty pans, mustard bullet, jugs, dredgers, sugar cutters, baking spittle, toasting forks, dripping pans, larkspits and preserving pots.

From the late 17th century improvements in education led to increased literacy and a growing thirst for knowledge. Books on every topic were eagerly snapped up and cookery books, which often included medical and brewing recipes, were extremely popular. Between 1700 and 1800 over 300 cookery titles were published, many of these going into several editions. In the early Georgian period these books were usually written by men who had served apprenticeships with French chefs working for royalty or the aristocracy. They included many French recipes

> '**So much is the blind Folly of this Age that [people] would rather be impos'd on by a French Booby, than give Encouragement to a good English Cook!**'
>
> Hannah Glasse

using expensive ingredients such as truffles and morels and were written in such old-fashioned language that they were difficult to understand. The attitude to French cooking was ambivalent: it was considered very fashionable to hire a French chef and yet they, and French food, were scoffed at.

It must be remembered that Britain was at war with France for a large part of the 18th century, and patriotism and the idea of true-born Englishmen were important. It was thought that the plain roast beef of old England made plain stalwart Englishmen.

Perhaps the preference for plainness is one reason why it is the cookery books written by women which succeeded so spectacularly, notably those by Eliza Smith (1st edition 1727), Hannah Glasse (1st edition 1747) and Elizabeth Raffald (1st edition 1769). Hannah Glasse's *The Art of Cookery made Plain and Easy* went into 17 editions between 1747 and 1803, and all other cookbooks pirated her recipes (as she herself had pirated from Eliza Smith and others). Mrs Glasse's recipes are more detailed in measures and method than those of her predecessors so that even an untutored cooking maid could understand them: 'I have attempted a Branch of Cookery which Nobody has yet thought worth their while to write upon... My Intention is to instruct the lower Sort [so that] every servant who can read will be capable of making a tolerable good Cook.'

As well as the preferred simplicity in cooking, these recipe books reflected the new standards of hygiene developed as a result of better education and the introduction of piped water to some towns. Mrs Glasse gives instructions on how to clean spits, gridirons, wooden bowls and other cooking utensils with sand and hot water only (soap would leave a flavour).

Bad meat, stale fish, rancid butter and spoiled fruit and vegetables were traps that lay in wait for the unwary shopper, and many cookery books had an important section on how to choose the best market stuff. They also had recipes on how to rescue bad meat with vinegar and spices – a rather dangerous practice. Hannah Glasse, for example, includes a recipe on how 'to save potted birds, that begin to be bad'.

Fresh food was kept in cellars or larders, but it could not be kept long – less than a week. As a result a great deal of preserving took place. Jams, pickles, fruit and vegetables were kept in glass or earthenware jars sealed with paper or leather; meat, fish and shellfish were potted under a layer of clarified butter; hams and bacon were cured; beef and mutton were salted and meats, fish, sausages and puddings were smoked over a wood or peat fire to preserve them. Ice was also used as a preserving agent and fashionable people built ice-houses in their grounds so that they could have ice available all year. One of the advantages of ice-houses was that the luxury of ice-creams could be enjoyed!

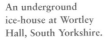

An underground ice-house at Wortley Hall, South Yorkshire.

VICTORIAN INDUSTRY AND IMAGINATION

In a poor home at the beginning of the 19th century, the fire was still set on a raised slab against a wall and fuelled by wood, peat or gorse. A cauldron hung by an iron chain or rod from a bar in the chimney or it might be perched on the fire resting on its three stubby legs. This container was often used for boiling 'stirabout', a plain or flavoured porridge that was often all a poor family could afford. The poor housewife did not fry or broil for lack of fat and if she roasted at all, this was done from a simple pot hook or else the meat was hung in a worsted cloth in front of the fire with a dish under it to catch the meat juices.

Oatcakes or small loaves might be baked on the hearth on a flat hot bakestone and a beehive-shaped portable earthenware oven was sometimes still used even at this period. However, many people living in the country sent their dough or pies to the communal village oven to be baked. City cookshops and bakers would roast or bake items for a small charge.

In a more affluent home, the fire was in a grate and fuelled by coal. Meat was broiled in a cast-iron frying pan or on a griddle with a long handle and boiling was done in cast-iron pots raised and lowered by a ratchet or a chimney crane. Meat or poultry were still roasted over the fire and the spits, and the mechanisms for turning them, were almost identical to those used in the Georgian period. Spit-roasting survived even after gas

Opposite The range was the focal point of the Victorian kitchen. *Below* The Charing Cross Kitchener, 1890, an early example of a gas cooker.

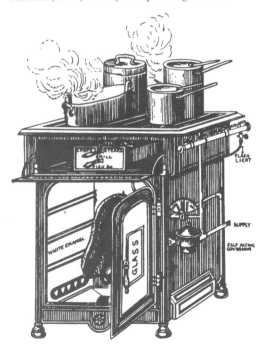

ovens were introduced as many people agreed with the cookbook editor who commented in 1886 that oven-roasted meat did not have the same succulent flavour.

By the beginning of the Victorian period most upper- and middle-class kitchens had a cast-iron oven or 'Yorkshire' range built into one side of the fireplace, though the fire was still open for roasting and toasting. However the 'Kitchener' range patented in 1802 quickly became popular in affluent homes in southern England because the cook could boil, fry and bake at the same time. However, it was expensive to buy, very hard work to keep clean and a glutton for fuel. North-country people stuck to the open range and poor people everywhere still cooked on a small open grate by balancing a kettle, frying pan or saucepan on the top.

In the early 19th century experiments had been made with gas cookers, but it was not until the 1880s that they became popular. By this time the gas companies were able to offer a very efficient and well-tested product which had wipe-down surfaces of vitreous enamel to make cleaning easier and well-insulated ovens with see-through doors – although the temperature still had to be guessed. Another new development was the grill which cooked food placed under it – this replaced the old gridirons which cooked food over the heat. Gas was readily available and

Opposite Cast-iron and copper pots and pans.
Below A busy kitchen at the Tower Bridge Hotel in Southwark, London, in 1897.

penny-in-the-slot gas meters let even relatively poor people use it. Gas cookers could also be hired quite cheaply and so by 1898, one home in four with a gas supply had a cooker as well.

The first electric power station for domestic consumers did not open until the 1880s, and though electric cookers were being demonstrated in the 1890s along with other electrical cooking equipment, their history really belongs to the 20th century.

The development of the closed cast-iron cooking range changed the shape of cooking pots and pans as they now needed to be flat-bottomed with shorter handles. They also got smaller because the range could hold more of them and, as fancy cooking became popular with the rising middle class, they became more specialised. A mid-Victorian cook might have omelette, sauté and frying pans, separate fish kettles for flat and round fish, and for salmon. Luckily for her, these were no longer made of copper or brass which needed hard scouring, but of tin-plated cast iron varnished black. Towards the end of the century, vitreous enamel began to be used as a finish and lightweight aluminium cookware first appeared.

Ladles, spoons, chopping knives, mashers, herb choppers and other traditional implements did not change, but a number of more specialised tools and gadgets were added to them, many of them metal versions of earlier ones. Mass-produced tinware, including pastry and biscuit cutters, patty pans, pikelet rings and jelly moulds, flooded middle-class kitchens. A boiled tongue could be curled up and pressed in a tinplate screw-down device like a cheese-press while biscuit and sweet tins, often gaudily painted, replaced bottles, jars and wooden boxes. The essential tin-opener was introduced during the 1860s to open cans of corned beef.

Free-standing toasters of various shapes were used to make some of the more delicate and elaborate dishes eaten at formal dinners. A common type was a tripod with a multi-pronged attachment and a drip-tray beneath which could be used for cooking small birds, fruits, nuts or cheese, as well as for toasting bread.

After 1865, tinned cast iron and tinplate were combined in many mechanical labour-saving gadgets such as a grater, bread rasper, potato peeler, mincer, bean slicer, marmalade cutter, knife sharpener and an enormous complicated apple corer, peeler and slicer. There was even a chopper and mixer – but no blender.

Food was kept fresh with liberal quantities of ice which was still stored underground or in well-insulated ice-houses. The trouble was that the ice quickly melted when it was brought into the house, though this problem was partly solved around 1840 when tin- or zinc-lined ice-chests began to appear. Once these were packed with ice, food could be placed inside and kept fresh for several days. About 15 years later a similar ice-chest was patented with an aerated compartment at the top for crushed ice, a drainage system for melted ice-water and a chilled lower compartment for food. The prototype refrigerator, which it was called, had been created.

The sorbets, ice creams and iced puddings which had become immensely popular for formal upper- and rising middle-class dinners since Georgian times could not be frozen in a small quantity of crushed ice alone. Experiments in making artificial ice led to the discovery that ice mixed with saltpetre or salt made a colder, longer-lasting freezing mixture. In about 1864 experiments in America showed that churning ice cream while it froze improved its texture and so ice-cream makers were developed which were like a pail with a cylinder inside which could be cranked by a handle. In later models, a paddle inside the cream container was worked by turning a handle.

Victorian cookery was not unlike that of today – except that the cook still prepared her own meat, fowl and fish as well as kneading, mixing and whisking by hand. Her gadgets were still clumsier than her fingers.

Opposite One of the many new gadgets available to the Victorian cook.
Below Advertisement for a patent ice-cream maker.

34   *Advertisements.*

BY ROYAL LETTERS PATENT.
MARSHALL'S PATENT FREEZER.

Complete View.

IS PRAISED BY ALL WHO KNOW IT FOR

CHEAPNESS in first cost.   CLEANLINESS in working.
ECONOMY in use.   SIMPLICITY in construction.
RAPIDITY in freezing.
NO PACKING NECESSARY.   NO SPATULA NECESSARY
Smooth and delicious Ice produced in 3 minutes.
SIZES—No. 1, to freeze any quantity up to 1 qt., £1 5 0. No. 2, for
wo qts., £1 15 0. No. 3, for four qts., £3 0 0. No. 4, for six qts.,
£4 0 0.   Larger sizes to order.

*The serving and eating of food –
etiquette, manners and tableware*

OSTENTATION, INDULGENCE AND EXTRAVAGANCE

Surviving records of Roman banquets provide a vivid insight into the extravagant aspirations and achievements of their cooks and reveal that the Romans often put more emphasis on the presentation and ostentation of their banquets rather than the taste of the food! At one recorded meal, the menu consisted of 600 ostrich brains, peas mixed with grains of gold, lentils mixed with precious stones and other dishes mixed with pearls and amber.

The Roman dining room was known as the *triclinium*, so called because it was usual to arrange three couches around a central dining table leaving the fourth side open for the serving slaves. Each couch could accommodate three reclining people who then rested their left arm on a cushion. The guests brought their own napkins with them to wear round their necks during the meal and to clean their face and fingers between courses, and slaves replaced the guests' shoes with sandals. After Jupiter and the household gods Penates and Lares had been invoked, the food arrived – the first course was an hors d'oeuvres; the second was the *coena* or meal proper; and the third course was a dessert which usually consisted of fresh or dried fruit, pastries or honey cakes. Between courses musicians, dancers, acrobats, clowns and even gladiators might appear to entertain the guests.

Although the Romans ate much of their food with their fingers, they did have cutlery in the form of knives and spoons –

A selection of knives used in Roman cookery.

Above An intricately decorated pewter flagon and handle.
Opposite A variety of copper cooking utensils.
Below A large Samian ware bowl from Aldborough
Roman Site in North Yorkshire.

but no forks. Knives were made in all sizes with iron or bronze blades and wood, bone or bronze handles. Spoons, used for eating soft foods and sauces, were made from silver, bronze or bone with round or oval bowls. A small spoon known as a *cocleare* was used for eating eggs with the bowl end and for picking shellfish out of their shells with the pointed handle. The round-bowled spoons are the earliest types while the lyre-shaped, oval bowl forms predominated in the 3rd and 4th centuries. Larger spoons and ladles of bronze or iron may have been used for serving food.

Equipment for serving wine was often very elaborate. Sometimes imported, it included special strainers, silver jugs, dishes, cups and goblets and enamelled wine ladles, cups and finger bowls.

The furnishings of the table and the interior decor of the dining room indicated social standing. Dining tables were sometimes equipped with ornate lamps, candelabra and sets of heated dishes as well as pewter or silver plates. The most exotic found in Britain are from the magnificent Mildenhall treasure which was probably intended for show rather than use. In contrast Red Samian ware pottery, imported from France, was used a great deal. There are two forms: large bowls with decoration in relief and a range of smaller bowls and platters which are undecorated.

Glass was much less common than pottery but included bowls, beakers, bottles and jugs which were usually made of a pale greenish colour. However, white, amber, blue and yellowish-green glass are also known and there are a few examples of the later polychrome glass from Roman London.

Two forms of metal jug have been found made in either pewter or bronze – a rather bulky, wide-mouthed jug with a broad

neck which merges into the body and a more graceful, relatively narrow-necked form which has its neck clearly separated from its bulbous body by a line of decoration. Such beautiful and elegant items were put to good use in the elaborate meals and banquets enjoyed during the Roman period.

Trimalchio's banquet, described by the satirist Petronius, gives an impression of the scale of such feasts. The first course was an hors d'oeuvres which included a bronze statue of a horse carrying panniers filled with olives; bridge-shaped salvers containing dormice; sizzling sausages and pomegranate seeds. Also on the table was a nest with a carved wooden hen sitting on pea-fowl eggs which were made of pastry enclosing spiced garden warblers. Crystal flagons of 100-year-old Falernian Opimian wine were opened for the guests to enjoy. The second course was served on a globe-shaped tray with the 12 signs of the Zodiac reproduced on its rim.

Above each sign were dishes which, in their shape or nature, had some link with the particular constellation. For example, Taurus had a piece of beef; Gemini kidneys and testicles and Libra a pair of scales with a pie on one side and a cake on the other. When the top of the globe was removed plump chickens, sows' udders and a hare with wings fastened to its back to symbolise Pegasus were revealed. Later there was wild boar with live thrushes in its belly and a huge pig cooked with sausages and black puddings inside it.

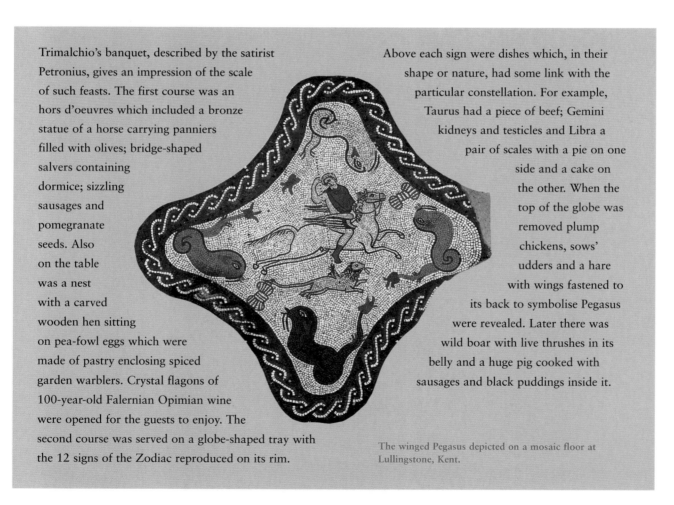

The winged Pegasus depicted on a mosaic floor at Lullingstone, Kent.

KNOWING YOUR PLACE IN THE MIDDLE AGES

The way the usual two-course dinner was conducted in a medieval manorial household was important to everyone who took part. Whether he was serving or sat in the lowest seat, it showed that he had a rightful, allotted place in this intricate hierarchy of working and social life, with both duties and customary rights.

When at home, the lord of the manor dined with his household in his great hall. It was always a formal meal to some degree in order to show his status, but he would generally hear requests and complaints before or after the meal as well as hand out the odd favour or rebuke. It helped everyone to know more or less where he or she stood.

How well this worked depended on the lord's status. The king or an archbishop dined in state every day and only great nobles or prelates could get near them but a good lesser lord was usually approachable – except at a feast which was mainly an occasion for display and entertainment.

More information is known about medieval feasts than ordinary dinners because the method of serving, seating arrangements and menus of some of them were recorded in detail at the time. However, the general plan of ordinary meals would have been much the same though the procedures were simplified.

At one end of the long hall was a raised platform or dais on which the lord, his family and his visitors were seated. They were

placed along one side of the table facing the room and the musicians' gallery at the other end with the lord sitting in the centre. Tables were set along the length of the hall on both sides to seat the household and lesser guests in order of rank. The table nearest the dais on the lord's right was the most important and it was called the 'Rewarde' as it was served with dishes from the lord's own table. The table opposite it was called the 'Second Messe' and the rest were graded similarly. At a large feast, there might be so many guests that tables had to be set in several rooms including the gallery.

Under the gallery, behind screens, were doors leading to the kitchen, buttery, cellar and pantry and near them were serving tables called 'cubberdes' (cupboards). At one side, or in an adjoining room, there was a 'ewery' with basins for hand-washing before the meal.

A few regular items, such as trencher bread, were common to everyone but, apart from these, different dishes had to be prepared for each table in the hall – with more for the top tables than others. Then, at least once a week, most of the dishes had to exclude meat (including meat-thickened sauces) and, since both raw and cooked meat might 'go off' between Thursday and Sunday, butchering had to be carefully planned to leave as few leftovers as possible on Thursday night.

There were also special groups of people to be fed. Medical teaching of the time stated that young children should have quite a different diet from adults – they were allowed milk but red meat and fruit were excluded. Then, even in a modest manor, there were several other groups of diners including a wholly separate one formed by the clergy.

A medieval illustration of King Richard II dining with the Dukes of York, Gloucester and Ireland.

'She leet no morsel from
   hir lippes falle,
Ne wette hir fingres in
   hir sauce depe.
Wel coude she carie a
   morsel, and wel kepe,
That no drope ne fille
   up-on hire brest.
In curteisye was set ful
   muche hir lest.'

Geoffrey Chaucer, *c.*1340-1400,
Prologue; Canterbury Tales,
description of the Prioress

Any menu was served in two main courses with a dessert course afterwards for special guests at a feast. Each course consisted of a number of poultry, meat or fish dishes and two or three sweet ones which were served to those at the high table and then put on the other tables for people to help themselves. Each dish was divided up beforehand and people shared a portion or 'messe' by either eating it from the shared platter or transferring bits to their trenchers. Sometimes cups were shared too.

A feast might have three courses and at the end of each one a carved hard-sugar sculpture known as a 'sotelte' was presented to the high table. Everyone had a chance to admire it and, if it was edible, they might even get a taste. When the table had been relaid for the second course, a procession might bring in a decorated peacock or swan and later the lord would give presents to his main guests.

The highest-ranking nobles had a steward who ran the household. Under him in order of importance, was the marshal and next in rank, in charge of different aspects of the meal, were: the sewer (head waiter and taster); the pantler or panter (head of the pantry); the butler (in charge of drinks); the ewerer (in charge of hand-washing and linen); the chief cook; the carver and the lord's cupbearer. Except for the last two, these all had several grooms (trained staff) and underlings to help them and there were also waiters, assistant waiters who brought the food only as far as the hall, assistant cooks, scullions, spit-boys, pot-boys and bottle-washers.

The household officials always laid the tables. First, the senior ewerer laid two or three cloths on the tables and set out a cloth and special basin for the lord and a cup for tasting the water.

Next, the pantler brought the lord's bread rolls wrapped in a napkin, his trenchers and the large ceremonial covered salt-cellar as well as a spoon and special knives for cutting the bread. He laid each one in a particular place in front of his master and then ensured that the other tables were provided with bread, trenchers, knives, spoons and trenchers for salt.

When the cooks were ready the company assembled but only the lord sat down. Everyone else went off to wash with the sewer, carver and cupbearer going first with towels and napkins elaborately draped over their shoulders. Then the assay or tasting ritual took place; advancing towards his master with three bows, the carver went down on his knees, uncovered and moved the salt, unwrapped the lord's bread, and cut a small cone of both white and trencher bread for the pantler to taste. At the same time, the marshal and cupbearer came forward with the lord's hand-washing basin, tasted the water and kissed the towel he should use. The first course was on the serving tables by this time, and the sewer gave a little of each dish to the chief cook and the lord's chief steward to taste for fear of poison.

Once these tastings had been done, lesser guests sat down in their places and the carver began his duty. There were elaborate medieval instructions for dressing and carving the various meats and birds with each one needing different handling – a skilled carver prided himself on the speed and dexterity of his performance. Once he had completed his task, the first course could at last be served.

Only one thing remained to be tasted and that was the drink. This was the job of the marshal, butler and cupbearer and was performed with the same flourishes as the food tasting. The

The carver at work on a nobleman's dinner in 1415. From the *Book of Hours of the Duke of Berry.*

tasting and serving of the ale, and wine for senior ranks, was timed to coincide with the serving of the first roast.

It was perhaps as well that senior officials tasted so many dishes because they now had to remain on their feet throughout the meal to ensure that everyone was served properly; that no important guest was left with an empty cup or a soiled trencher, and that each dish was served with the right sauce. Then, when the meal had ended, the tables were cleared and, if the lord had guests, sweet wine was served with wafers and whole spices as dessert. Finally, grace was said and the lord got on his feet to drink a toast as a signal that dinner was over and that everyone should go back to work.

Manners, cleanliness and courtesy were considered so important both for the enjoyment of food and for communal living generally that instructions were painstakingly written down for generations of lords and ladies in the making to learn. Most of these etiquette books gave instructions about personal cleanliness and how to share a 'messe' courteously with other people. A young guest was told to have clean nails and not make greasy fingermarks on the table; he must not drink from a shared cup with his mouth full nor drink his soup noisily, and he should not pick his teeth with his knife, blow on his food to cool it or wipe his mouth on the tablecloth. For his neighbour's sake he should clean his spoon properly and not leave it in the dish and he should not dip his fingers too deep in the shared dish, nor crumble bread into it in case his hands were sweaty. He should definitely not gnaw bones nor tear

Dinner in the 15th century. The cupbearer approaches the lady of the house and, under the balcony, the steward keeps an eye on the household servants.

meat to bits with his teeth or fingers. Scratching his head at table was also unacceptable and there were other specific instructions about how, when and where to spit and belch.

These basic directions seem a curious contrast to the fanciful etiquette of preparing the table, tasting and serving. But even a manorial household or similar group still consisted largely of people with a peasant and farming background – even lordlings had been brought up in close contact with peasant life.

'Pyke not thine Eris ne thy nostrellis: If thou do, men wolle sey thou come of cherlis.'

Anon, *The Little Children's Little Book,*
*c.*1480

POMP, CEREMONY AND BANQUETING HOUSES

In most establishments the full medieval ceremonials, menus, courses and methods of service continued virtually unchanged throughout the 16th century. However, royal and very wealthy households introduced one different but very significant detail: instead of dining at the head of the entire household in the great hall, the lord, his family and the officers who served him at table, now withdrew into their more private great chambers or 'dining chambers' – though they still dined in the hall on important occasions such as royal visits, weddings and Christmas. There was also a tendency to decrease and regulate the number of meals served during the day: 'Whereas of old we had breakfasts in the forenoon, beverages or nunchions after dinner, and thereto rear-suppers, generally when it was time to go to rest, now these odd repasts, thanked be to God, are very well left, and each one in manner contenteth himself with dinner and supper only.' For the gentry, dinner was served at eleven in the morning and supper between five and six in the evening but on special occasions these meals could be extended by 'banquets'.

The Tudor meaning of the word 'banquet' was different from the present-day understanding – in its original 16th-century form the banquet was an elaborate dessert course of sweetmeats, fruits and wine. This was served either as a meal in itself or as a continuation of dinner or supper and it was set out in a separate

An elaborate 'marchpane' – a coloured marzipan confection – in the shape of a Tudor rose.

apartment. After the main meal had been cleared from the Presence Chamber at York Place (now St James's Palace) a group of masquers disguised as shepherds entered with a flourish of hautboys. As Cardinal Wolsey recognised Henry VIII among the unexpected party, he called to Sir Thomas Lovell (Chancellor of the Exchequer and Treasurer of the King's Household), 'Is the banquet ready i'th Privy Chamber?' While Wolsey retired to his Privy Chamber to enjoy this dessert course, other noble hosts might go up to the ornate banqueting houses erected on the roofs of their houses such as those at Longleat, Hardwick or Lacock Abbey – or perhaps proceed to delightful banqueting houses or lodges erected in some secluded corner of their parks. These might be permanent structures but often they were 'made with fir poles and decked with birch branches and all manner of flowers both of the field and of the garden, as roses, julyflowers, lavender, marygolds, and all manner of strewing herbs and rushes' like the one Queen Elizabeth I ordered to be built in Greenwich Park for the reception of the French Embassy in 1560.

The banquet provided the greatest opportunity for the display of wealth, colour, ingenuity and culinary splendour. At Kenilworth, Robert Dudley's entertainment for the queen featured 'a most delicious and an ambrosial banquet; whereof whether I might muse at the daintiness, shapes, and the cost, or else, at the variety and number of the dishes (that were three hundred)'. *The Good Huswife's Closet* gives detailed instructions of how to make all kinds of banqueting dishes, including three-dimensional birds, beasts and fruits in spun sugar or pies and baskets in marzipan. Even the wine glasses, dishes, playing cards and trenchers were made of a crisp, modelled sugar called sugar-plate which could be

Elizabeth I takes
breakfast before the
hunt, 1575.

elaborately painted and embellished with bright gilding. Although all the sugar-plate trenchers disappeared centuries ago, wooden versions made from sycamore have survived: these are decorated on one side with floral and strapwork motifs and a suitable inscription. George Puttenham's *Art of English Poesie* of 1589 describes

> *Epigrams that were sent usually for New Yeares gifts or to be printed or put upon their banketting dishes of sugar plate or of March paines ... they were called "Apophereta" and never contained above one verse or two at the most, but the shorter the better. We call them poesies, and do paint them now a dayes upon the backe sides of our fruit trenchers of wood.*

In addition to taking part in outdoor banquets, the Tudor monarchs also enjoyed the elaborate breakfasts which preceded the hunt. The English were known throughout Europe for their love of field sports, and most of the royal palaces and great houses had a deer park dotted with trees and enclosed by a high wooden fence. While visiting Viscount Montagu, Elizabeth I rode out into the park where a delicate bower had been prepared for her reception. On these hunting days the preparations for the entertainment of the queen started when the butler set off into the park with a train of waggons, carts and pack-mules carrying all the necessary food and drink to the place of assembly. This location was carefully chosen to ensure adequate shade beneath stately trees, an array of wild flowers, a nearby spring of clear water and sweet singing birds. The butler's first task was to place bottles and barrels of beer and wine into the spring to cool.

That doone: he spreades his cloth, upon the grassye banke,
And sets to shewe his deintie drinkes, to winne his Princes
    thanke.
Then commes the captain Cooke, with many a warlike wight,
Which armor bring and weapons both, with hunger for to
    fight ...
For whiles colde loynes of Veale, cold Capon, Beefe and
    Goose,
With Pygeon pyes, and Mutton colde, are set on hunger
    loose ...
First Neates tongs poudred well, and Gambones of the Hogge,
Then Saulsages and savery knacke, to set mens myndes on
    gogge ...
Then King or comely Queene, then Lord and Lady looke,
To see which side will bear the bell, the Butler or the Cooke.
At last the Cooke takes flight, the Butlers still abyde,
And sound their Drummes and make retreat, with bottles
    by their syde.'

The assembled hunters then presented the queen with accounts
of the various deer they had located, together with samples of
droppings, so that she might select the quarry for the day – and
so the hunt began.

Wherever the meal was to be served, the tableware used in
royal and noble households was always of the finest quality.
Following the medieval tradition, the great continued to eat and
drink from vessels made of gold, silver-gilt or silver. These were as
much for show as for use: Henry VIII displayed a cupboard of 12
shelves all filled with plate of gold at his feasts while George

An elaborate salt cellar made in London in 1562.

Cavendish, in his *Life of Cardinal Wolsey*, described the proud prelate's 'Cup Board made for the Chamber, in length of the breadth of the nether end of the same Chamber, six desks [ie shelves] high, full of gold plate, very sumptuous, and of the newest fashions, and upon the nethermost desk garnished all with gold, most curiously wrought … This Cup Board was barred in round about that no man might come nigh it.' The number of shelves was quite significant – dukes being permitted four or five, lesser noblemen three, knights two and ordinary gentlemen one.

On the table, pride of place was still occupied by the great salt which was the first vessel to be set in place and the principal decoration. In shape it could vary considerably, but it was quite tall, raised on ornate feet with its gilt bowl surmounted by a high canopy or cover. Around the table much smaller salt cellars might also be provided for less important diners and members of the household.

The 16th century saw the decline of the medieval practice of serving food on square-cut trenchers made of wholemeal bread. Instead the bread was now used as sops which were put under boiled or stewed meats to soak up the gravy. The trencher changed its form and became a thin, square wooden board with recesses for meat and salt. Further changes in tableware occurred when Jasper Andries and Jacob Jansen left Antwerp in 1567 to establish tin-glazed earthenware potteries in Norwich and London. Unlike the native English wares, their products had a smooth, glossy white surface which could be painted with metallic oxides to give colourful permanent decoration in the most fashionable Renaissance style.

The materials and design of drinking vessels also made great leaps forward during this period. By 1500, the traditional ashwood drinking cups, which cost Henry VIII £20 a year to buy, were

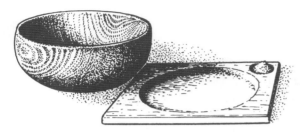

Wooden tableware was still in general use. Here is a wooden cup, identical to those used from the Viking period, while the square trencher, with its small hollow for salt, was of recent introduction, replacing earlier trenchers of coarse bread.

being replaced by earthenware cups. These were made in vast quantities in the south-east of England where Surrey kilns produced 'Tudor Green' forms with a brilliant copper-green glaze over a finely thrown creamy-buff pottery. In the northern counties the cups were made of a hard-fired dark red material which was glazed to a glossy dark brown or black and decorated with flowers, stags' heads and stamped pads of white clay. This type of pottery is known as Cistercian ware since it was first discovered during the excavation of Cistercian monasteries in Yorkshire.

Glass too was becoming increasingly widespread. In 1575 the Venetian Jacomo Verzelini left the Netherlands to establish a glasshouse in London. Here he began to produce bowls and glasses of the highest quality, their surfaces often elaborately engraved with the customer's coat of arms and initials. In the provinces, meanwhile, in Surrey and Sussex, the Bristol Channel area, Staffordshire, Lancashire, Cheshire and North Yorkshire, further glasshouses were soon employing local materials to make a wide range of goblets, bottles, distillation equipment and beer glasses. The last according to Sir Hugh Platt's *Jewell House of Art and Nature* were 'of six or eight inches in height and being of one equal bigness from the bottom to the top'.

Cutlery remained virtually unaltered in this period except for the slow introduction of the fork. Henry VIII had owned 'suckett' forks, with a spoon at one end and a two-pronged fork at the other end of a single shaft, while Elizabeth I began to receive new year gifts of gold and silver forks with rock-crystal handles from 1582. These were probably used to eat the sticky sweetmeats served at banquets and many more years were to pass before the fork came into general use in this country.

DINING ROOMS AND THE ACCEPTANCE OF THE FORK

Until the early years of the 17th century, the gentry lived within large households that included relations, chaplains, tutors, porters and an immense number of servants. In all but the grandest houses, they all dined together in the great hall. However, when the gentry started to spend more time in town and more money on personal pleasures, the old-fashioned extended household proved to be an expensive encumbrance and soon became a thing of the past.

Imitating the Elizabethan nobility, the gentry now abandoned the great hall for all but the largest social events and began to take their meals in a completely new setting – the dining room. In older houses the parlour, a private bed-sitting room, was often transformed into a dining room with new decorations and furniture while in new houses a purpose-built dining room was of the greatest importance. With its walls lined with elegant timber panelling or embossed, painted and gilded Cordovan goatskin, its plaster ceiling enriched with mouldings, its impressive fireplace and sumptuously curtained windows, the dining room provided an ideal setting in which to entertain guests and make a powerful display of wealth and taste.

From the middle of the 17th century dining rooms were furnished with a dining table, often of the oval, gate-legged variety, surrounded by a matching set of chairs for the most

'Strange to see how a good dinner and feasting reconciles everybody.'

Samuel Pepys, 1633–1703

important diners. A long table and a set of stools for other members of the household might also be provided, and livery cupboards or sideboards would be placed in the room to hold dishes of food as well as display gold, silver or fine pottery.

The table, when being prepared for a meal, was first covered with a fine linen cloth and then laid with all the required plates, salts and saucers. These were made of silver or silver-gilt in the larger houses as they provided a convenient and ostentatious way of storing wealth in a period when modern banking systems were still in their infancy. Although much early plate was melted down during the Civil War, there was a great revival in the use of silver tableware after the Restoration – for example, in 1670 Prince Rupert purchased five dozen silver plates from Alderman Blackwell at a cost of almost £300. The cost of keeping in fashion was very high! Much of this domestic plate was made in London where it found a ready market among the nobility and gentry who came up to town for the winter season, but major regional centres such as Newcastle, York, Chester, Norwich and Exeter also produced silverware of the highest standard.

Since solid silver was so expensive, many households used pewter as a substitute as it looked like silver when polished. Composed of tin, with a small percentage of lead and copper, pewter cost only 1s to 1s 2d a pound and therefore could be used in much greater quantities by a far wider section of the community. It was, however, easily damaged as the metal was so soft that a hard cut with a knife would score its surface quite deeply – such marks had to be burnished over or polished out using fine abrasive sand.

This troublesome operation could be avoided by using delftware made of a light biscuit-coloured pottery covered in a smooth and glossy opaque white glaze. Made in England since the late 1560s, it now enjoyed great popularity. Production was centred in the London parishes of Aldgate and Southwark and, from the mid-17th century, at Brislington near Bristol. Many pieces were decorated with blue brushwork in the Chinese manner, imitating Ming or 'Transitional' porcelain, while others, particularly the large 'blue-dash chargers' (so-called from the decoration around their rims), were painted with brightly coloured flowers, portraits, or pictures of Adam and Eve. English lead-glazed earthenware also made great advances from the mid-17th century. By the 1660s the supremacy of the Staffordshire potters had already become fully established, their slipwares decorated in coloured liquid clays being particularly attractive. Thomas Toft was particularly celebrated for his great dishes decorated with lively royal portraits or coats of arms which provided appropriately loyal images for the dining room.

In many households wooden tableware was still in use, the square wooden trencher with its shallow recesses now being replaced by circular wooden plates or platters. Large communal drinking bowls still survived too, but from the end of Elizabeth I's reign glassware had become much more common, appearing in the form of wine glasses, tumblers, and a range of sweetmeat, jelly and syllabub glasses.

The most significant change in tableware was the emergence of the fork as a major item of cutlery from the early 17th century, when it was popularised by the writer Thomas Coryate. He published an account of its use in Italy in 1611.

Half a century was to pass before forks were generally accepted, but by the 1660s sets of knives and forks were being

'Forks? What be they?'
'The laudable use of forks,
Brought into custom here,
as they are in Italy,
To the sparing of napkins.'

Ben Jonson, 1616

made. The knife now adopted a rounded end, in contrast to its earlier pointed form which had been necessary when it had to spear meat from the dishes.

At this period the day was punctuated by three main meals: breakfast, taken shortly after rising; dinner, taken at midday; and supper, taken in the early evening. The first of these was a relatively light meal by the standards of the day, probably, by the end of the century, consisting of a selection of cold meats, bread and butter, and cakes served with tea, coffee or chocolate. However, then – as now – there were great contrasts in breakfast preferences.

Unlike today's dinners, in which the frequent courses follow each other in a set sequence from soup to dessert, the 17th-century dinner consisted of two or three courses each comprising a number of different sweet and savoury dishes. The diner could help himself to whatever he liked in the manner of a modern buffet, thus giving each individual much greater freedom of choice. The first course would be placed on the table in a neat, symmetrical arrangement and would include most of the major meat dishes as well as soups which would be

An elegant dinner of seven and nine dishes.

removed and their place taken by a further dish once everyone had been served. In the second course there would be a range of lighter meats, game and sweet dishes laid in a similar symmetrical pattern, but this division was only a general rule, leaving plenty of scope to include whatever might be available at any particular time. The third course was composed of fruit, sweets and cheese, but the manner in which it was served changed during the 17th century. During the earlier decades it continued in the form of the Elizabethan banquet, allowing the cooks and the gardeners to

make a great show of their skills with elaborate confections and rare fruits displayed in new and exciting ways. For important functions, cardboard galleons sailing on seas of salt could startle guests with their cannon, fired with real gunpowder, while pastry deer bled red wine when arrows were pulled from their sides. John Evelyn gives the following colourful account of William and Mary's entertainment for the Venetian ambassadors, when 'the banquet was twelve vast chargers piled up so high that those that sat one against another could hardly see each other. Of these, sweetmeats, which doubtless took some days piling up in this exquisite manner, the Ambassadors touched

'1662

March 26th. I had a pretty dinner for them, viz. a brace of stewed carps, six roasted chickens, and a jowl of salmon, hot, for the first course; a tanzy (a pudding, named after the herb tansy which was used for making puddings) and two neats' tongues, and cheese the second; and were very merry in the afternoon, talking and singing and piping upon the flageolette.'

Samuel Pepys, 1633–1703

not, but left them to the spectators … in a moment of time all that curious work was demolished, the confitures voided, and the tables cleared.' This appears to have been the fate of many royal banquets. Even when the Garter knights held their great dinner in the magnificent Banqueting House in Whitehall, 'the banqueting-stuff was flung around the room profusely'. In most households, however, particularly from the Restoration, the third course gradually began to be served at the dining table, in the manner of a modern dessert.

Only a single course was laid for supper but it could be made up of numerous dishes, or be extended by a banquet whenever necessary. After a few hours of good conversation, music, singing and cards, accompanied by much alcohol and, perhaps, tobacco, the company would be served with a light meal to prepare them for their homeward journey or for the chill of the bedroom – Pepys, for example, having 'a good sack-posset and cold meat and sent my guests away about 10-a-clock at night'. The sack posset certainly provided the ideal close to the day: made of eggs, wine and spices scalded with sweetened cream, spooned from the most beautifully decorated silverware or sipped from voluminous earthenware vessels, its rich, smooth warmth and alcoholic potency soon lulled the diners into total oblivion. 'And so to bed.'

AFTERNOON TEA AND 'FRENCH EASE'

During the Georgian period the times of meals gradually began to change. In the early 18th century the middle classes and the higher orders might breakfast at 9 or 10 am and have nothing else before dinner which was usually at 2 or 3 pm. As the century progressed dinner was served later so that by the late 18th century it was generally at 6 or 7 pm. This left a long gap which was filled by the new development of afternoon tea. The less fashionable classes who continued to have dinner in the middle of the day had a dish of tea in the afternoon, then a supper of cold meats, cold pies, bread and cheese in the evening.

Many cookery books from this period include diagrams of dinner-table layouts, which vary from the modest to the lavish . As in Stuart times, the dishes for each course were placed very correctly and symmetrically on the table. The type of food eaten at each course had also changed little but by now the dessert was always served in the dining room. After the dessert had been removed, and a glass or two of wine drunk, the ladies withdrew and left the men to their drinking. The men would join the ladies for conversation or card games later in the evening.

Rules for behaviour during the meals were set out by John Trusler in *The Honours of the Table*, published in 1788. Guests were to walk into the dining room in strict order of rank with ladies first. The mistress of the house sat at the top end of the

In his satirical handbook *Directions to Servants*, 1745, Jonathan Swift 'recommends' bad, slovenly practices inferring that servants had subtle ways of getting even with their masters and mistresses. For instance, he tells the cook, if her mistress does not allow her the usual prerequisite of the dripping, to use it now and then along with expensive butter to enliven the fire. He also suggests taking half the meat to share with the butler in exchange for the butler's wine; if a lump of soot falls down the chimney into the soup, to stir it into the soup to give it a high 'French' taste; if dinner is late to turn back the clock; to comb her hair while she is cooking and, if anyone complains about hair in the food, say it is the footman's; and if a chicken leg disappears to say a dog stole it.

'It is exceedingly rude to scratch any part of your body, to spit, or blow your nose ... to lean your elbows on the plate, to sit too far from it, to pick your teeth before the dishes are removed.'

John Trusler,
The Honours of the Table, 1788

table among all the women, with the most important female guests next to her, while her husband sat among the men in order of rank at the bottom end of the table. At the beginning of the 18th century the English hostess did all the carving and serving herself and so missed much of the food and the conversation. By mid-century, however, a new 'French ease' had become fashionable whereby the master and mistress carved the dishes that were before them at each end of the table. They served these to their guests who were then expected to help themselves and each other to the remainder of the dishes on the tables. By the turn of the 19th century, even this fashion had declined and food was now served by the servants.

Trusler provides instructions on how to behave during meals: it is vulgar to eat too quickly or too slowly which shows you are either too hungry or you don't like the food; it is also vulgar to eat your soup with your nose in the plate and you must avoid 'smelling to the meat whilst on the fork' as it shows you suspect the meat is tainted.

If the necessity of nature obliged you to leave the table, you had to steal away unobserved and return without announcing where you had been. Chamber pots had been kept in or just outside the dining room but the new delicacy of feelings shrank from such crudeness.

The 'morning room' at Saltram, a fine Georgian house near Plymouth in Devon.

LATE MEALS AND PROMISCUOUS SEATING

In the early Victorian period, breakfast was taken between 9 and 10 am as in the 18th century, but it became more substantial. The aristocratic 18th-century custom of having just chocolate, coffee or tea, toast and hot sweet rolls still held for some people, but a cooked breakfast was popular with men. Luncheon was still a light snack meal taken at about 1 o'clock to fill the gap between breakfast and the later dinner hour. This was rapidly getting even later because more and more men worked in their own or other people's offices.

A plain everyday dinner at home might consist of only three or four savoury dishes, with a couple of sweet dishes or cheese afterwards. A formal dinner, however, was still set out in 18th-century style in two or three courses – in fact, two complete self-service meals were served, one after the other.

Dishes and tableware remained virtually unchanged from their 18th-century shapes but there were some novelties. For instance, early in the 19th century it became fashionable to use silver servers, knives and forks for eating fish and fruit because it was thought that steel spoiled the flavour and acid foods corroded the metal. More importantly, bone china with its translucent body and sparkling glaze was developed to beautify dinner tables.

Two cloths were laid on the table for dinner, one for removal between courses or before the dessert – table mats, leaving the

MENU

Caviar Sur Croûtes
Croûte au Pot
Saumon bouilli,
Sauce Écrevisses
Côtelettes de Pigeon
à l'Américaine
Poulet à la Valencienne
Pommes de Terre frites
Épinards à la Crème
Iced Pudding à la Nesselrode
Dessert and Ices

table bare, now began to be used at lunch but never at dinner. An elegant centrepiece was placed in the middle of the table – this could be a 'plateau', a chased silver or glass oblong tray on small feet, or an 'épergne', a tall ornament with branches holding small dishes of sweetmeats, fruit or flowers. Later in the century this would often be replaced by a flower arrangement or by a 'tazza', a stemmed shallow bowl or plate like a cake-stand for fruit, sweetmeats or trailing floral decorations.

One marked change in dining habits occurred early in the 19th century. Instead of the ladies entering the room first in order of precedence, followed by the gentlemen, so that the sexes were seated separately, it became the custom for each lady to be escorted into dinner by a gentleman who then sat next to her. However, in spite of this 'promiscuous seating' as it was called, etiquette demanded that all the ladies should be served first as in the past; and from this grew the custom of every gentleman serving his lady companion before himself. As a lady may not ask for wine, he also had to make sure that she was served, both during and after dinner, with the wine she preferred. He was expected to call for the same wine for himself and, when the glasses came, bow to his companion and drink to her.

The number of different wines served during a meal now increased and so did the variety of glasses required. By the 1850s, a different wine would be served at each stage of the meal, each in a special glass, and these would be arrayed on the table beside each diner instead of being called for. 'Finger glasses' – the small glasses of water supplied before the dessert for rinsing out the mouth – were used for a different purpose in Victorian times. Early in the 19th century they began to be used instead to wet the

'It is not worth the while to live by rich cookery.'

Henry David Thoreau, 1817–62

corner of the napkin in order to wipe the mouth and then to rinse the fingertips.

Men still stayed drinking in the dining room long after dinner and their manners were as coarse as in the 18th century. Ladies stayed only after the dessert for perhaps two glasses of wine and then retired.

In the second half of the 19th century, three important changes took place in the eating patterns of well-to-do Victorians: mealtimes changed, meals became larger and more elaborate, and the serving system changed completely. As the pattern of 'going to the office' developed even further, breakfast got slightly earlier and dinner a lot later. A man might go to his club after his office day, before returning home to change his clothes and have one of the newly popular aperitifs. At a dinner party, the meal was seldom served before 8, 9 or even 10 pm.

The Victorian breakfast was a hearty affair. In 1861 Mrs Beeton suggested any cold joint in the larder might be placed 'nicely garnished' on the sideboard along with collared and potted meats or fish, cold game or poultry, veal and ham pies, game pies, cold ham and tongue – pressed in the new-style tin press. These were to supplement a choice of hot dishes, such as broiled mackerel or other fish, mutton chops and rump steaks, broiled sheeps' kidneys, sausages, bacon, eggs, muffins, toast, marmalade, butter, jam, tea and coffee. She suggested adding fruit in the summer.

Lunch was still quite light; the same cold dishes would do as at breakfast or a mother might eat the same hot meal as the children. If a woman entertained, the dishes would be dainty rather than filling, but this was not common, and she was more likely to have soup, or chicken sandwiches alone. However, if it

'The food of thy soul is light and space; feed it then on light and space. But the food of thy body is champagne and oysters; feed it then on champagne and oysters; and so shall it merit a joyful resurrection, if there is any to be.'

Herman Melville, 1819–91

was her 'At Home Day', she would serve afternoon tea with hot teacakes, thin sandwiches, an array of small cakes and biscuits and at least one large cake made with baking powder instead of yeast.

And then there was dinner. Well-to-do Victorians served prodigious quantities at a dinner party. Even a small dinner for six given by people of modest means in 1861 contained at least 13 dishes and dessert. Mrs Beeton, however, also suggests menus for 'Plain Family Dinners' such as bubble and squeak followed by baked semolina pudding.

Following French custom, a new way of serving meals had begun to creep in during the early 19th century although it was not really adopted in middle-class homes until the 1850s. Even Mrs Beeton was dubious about it. The new style consisted of sending one kind of dish up to the table at a time beginning with soup and fish, then made-up meat dishes (entrées), roasts, poultry and game, then vegetable and sweet dishes called entremets, and finally desserts. Fashionable dining also demanded that all the serving (including carving) had to now be done in the kitchen so that diners were issued with a ready-prepared plate. English hostesses wavered but finally, towards the end of the 19th century, settled for a compromise in which modern-style courses (soup, fish, etc) were sent to the table in turn, any carving was done at a side table, and the dish, or choice of dishes, was handed round to the diners.

What made such a dinner so very different from today was that there were usually six or seven courses and a choice – sometimes a very wide choice – in each. At a really long, large dinner, the cook might also serve an iced sorbet after the main course to revive the palate.

'If this is coffee, please bring me some tea; but if this is tea, please bring me some coffee.'

Abraham Lincoln, 1809–65

It was as well that serving dishes were now handed round because there was no room for them on the table among the clutter of assorted wine glasses, rows of knives and forks, tasse, vases of flowers, and napkins twisted into fancy shapes. All these were larger than before and more elaborate. The Victorians engraved, embossed, curled and chased every surface. Curiously, they standardised the shapes of cutlery, such as knife-blades and the tines of forks – the development of electroplated nickel silver tableware for modest homes in the latter part of the period encouraged this.

No mid-Victorian table would have been complete without a vase of flowers. Mrs Beeton stresses that one should even be placed on the breakfast table. At dinner parties, the height of the flower arrangements tended to make conversation across the table impossible but this hardly mattered since good manners demanded that polite conversation should be confined to one's neighbours.

By the 1850s, table manners had become genteel. Fish, for instance, had to be eaten with just a fork and a scrap of bread – the fish knife was only for toying with. Diners were expected to try each dish but only eat a little; it was no longer 'done' to wet the napkin to dab the mouth and ladies, especially, should only dabble their fingertips in the finger-bowl. It was not good manners to gulp down a glass of wine and gentlemen had to drink each different wine slowly until the ladies left the room and they could settle to their port – even then they were expected to appear in the drawing room quite soon after the ladies' coffee tray had been removed.

Between dinner parties, the average, reasonably affluent Victorian family lived relatively plainly. Nevertheless, by modern

A Victorian method of making a table napkin look decorative

The Mitre

Fold the napkin in three, lengthways

Fold the ends to the middle

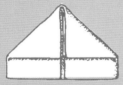

Fold over the top corners

Turn the folded napkin over, raise the outer corners and tuck into each other to form the finished mitre design

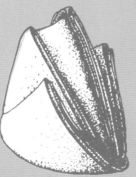

The Collegian

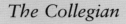

Fold the napkin in four, lengthways

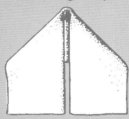

Turn down the ends diagonally from the centre

Turn the folded napkin over and roll up the ends

Turn the rolls under as indicated by the diagonal dotted lines shown above

The Victorian table napkin was a 30 inch square of starched and crisply ironed linen damask, which was folded into a variety of ornamental forms and set beside each place setting on the dining table

standards, they spent a disproportionate amount of their time thinking about food and drink, and in entertaining for show. A well-to-do married couple with business connections might give four dinner parties a month for 12 to 16 guests, and would serve 20 to 30 dishes each time. It was fortunate that their cook would now have had a mincer, bean slicer, bread rasper, wire egg whisk, packet jellies, custard powder, ice-box, freezer pail and above all her combination Kitchener to produce the showy dishes on the sparkling plate which these occasions required.

Left An épergne or table centre.
Opposite Painted glass at Brodsworth Hall, South Yorkshire.

The recipes

ROMAN RECIPES

Asafoetida: Available from chemists but use very sparingly.
Caroenum: A very sweet wine reduced by boiling to a third of its volume and mixed with honey.
Passum: A very sweet wine.

FISH COOKED IN ITS OWN JUICE

1 salmon, salmon trout or trout
15 ml (1 tbls) salt
15 ml (1 tbls) coriander seeds
15 ml (1 tbls) vinegar

Clean, wash and dry the fish. Pound the salt and the coriander seeds in a mortar. Roll the fish in this mixture. Place the fish in an ovenproof frying pan, seal by frying quickly on both sides, then cover with a lid. Put the pan in the oven and bake at gas mark 4, 180°C (350°F) until the fish is cooked through. Remove from the oven, sprinkle with strong vinegar.

BOILED MUSSELS

575–750 ml (1–1½ pt) mussels per person
a pinch of each of the following:
    celery seeds, rue, peppercorns
15 ml (1 tbls) honey
15 ml (1 tbls) *passum*
15 ml (1 tbls) olive oil
5 ml (1 tsp) anchovy essence
15 ml (1 tbls) cornflour

Prepare and cook the mussels by boiling. Remove from their shells and keep warm. Pound the celery seeds, rue, pepper and honey

together in a mortar. Add *passum*, olive oil and anchovy essence, and put in a pan. Blend in the cornflour and bring to the boil stirring all the time, until the sauce thickens. Pour over the mussels, sprinkle with pepper and serve.

OYSTERS

3–4 oysters per person
a pinch of pepper
a pinch of ground lovage
2 egg yolks
15 ml (1 tbls) vinegar
15 ml (1 tbls) olive oil
15 ml (1 tbls) wine
5 ml (1 tsp) anchovy essence
15 ml (1 tbls) honey (optional)

Ask your fishmonger to open the oyster shells, as near as possible to the time of eating. They can then be served raw or stewed or baked, covered with the following sauce. Mix the pepper and lovage with the egg yolks, then add the vinegar, a drop at a time, to make a smooth mixture. Stir in the olive oil, wine, anchovy essence and honey if using. Mix all thoroughly together, pour over the oysters and serve.

PRAWN RISSOLES

24 cooked shelled prawns
a pinch of pepper
5 ml (1 tsp) anchovy essence
1 egg, beaten
flour

Pound the prawns in a mortar with the pepper and anchovy essence. Mix in the beaten egg to bind and form into rissoles. Roll in flour and fry gently in oil until lightly browned on both sides.

MILK-FED SNAILS

6 edible snails per person
1 litre (1³/₄ pt) milk
salt
To serve:
5 ml (1 tsp) anchovy essence
15 ml (1 tbls) wine

Clean the snails with a sponge and remove the membranes so that they can come out of their shells. Put in a vessel with half the milk and salt for 1 day, then in a fresh vessel with the remaining milk for 1 more day, cleaning away the excrement every hour. When the snails are fattened to the point where they cannot return to their shells, fry them in oil. Serve with a dressing of anchovy essence and wine.

SUCKING PIG À LA FLACCUS

1 sucking pig
salt
a pinch of each of the following:
    pepper, lovage, caraway seeds,
    celery seeds, rue
1 drop *asafoetida* essence
5 ml (1 tsp) anchovy essence
45 ml (3 tbls) wine
15 ml (1 tbls) *passum*
10 ml (2 tsps) olive oil
15 ml (1 tbls) cornflour
To serve:
ground celery seeds

Clean the pig. Sprinkle with salt and roast at gas mark 4, 180°C (350°F) allowing 25 minutes per 450 g (1 lb) plus 25 minutes. While it is cooking, pound the pepper, lovage, caraway, celery seeds and rue in a mortar. Moisten with *asafoetida* essence and anchovy essence, then blend in the wine and *passum*. Put in a saucepan with the olive oil and bring to the boil. Thicken with cornflour mixed with water. Add the juices from the roast sucking pig, bring to the boil and simmer gently until thickened. Pour over the pig, and sprinkle with ground celery seeds. Serve hot.

SAUCE FOR MEAT SLICES

A pinch of each of the following:
    pepper, lovage, caraway seeds, dried
    mint, spikenard
1 egg yolk
15 ml (1 tbls) honey
15 ml (1 tbls) vinegar
15 ml (1 tbls) olive oil
5 ml (1 tsp) anchovy essence
1 bay leaf
1 leek (optional)
15 ml (1 tbls) cornflour

Pound the pepper, lovage, caraway, mint and spikenard in a mortar, then mix together with the egg yolk, honey, vinegar, olive oil and anchovy essence. Place in a pan over a low heat, and add the bay leaf. A leek may also be added for extra flavour if desired. Blend in the cornflour and stir until thickened. Remove leek and bay leaf and pour immediately over the meat slices.

STUFFED HARE

1 hare
225 g (8 oz) whole pine kernels
100 g (4 oz) shelled almonds
100 g (4 oz) chopped mixed nuts
25 g (1 oz) peppercorns
2 eggs, beaten
a pinch of each of the following:
    pepper, rue, savory
1 small onion, chopped
100 g (4 oz) stoned dates
5 ml (1 tsp) anchovy essence
30 ml (2 tbls) spiced wine

Mix together the pine kernels, almonds, chopped mixed nuts, peppercorns and add the chopped giblets of the hare. Bind with the eggs and use the mixture to stuff the hare. Wrap the hare in baking foil and roast in the oven at gas mark 5, 190°C (375°F) for 1–1½ hours until tender. To make the sauce: Put the pepper, rue, savory, chopped onion, dates, anchovy essence, spiced wine and the juices from the roast hare in a saucepan. Let this boil gently until thickened and serve with the hare.

SAUCE FOR ROAST WOOD PIGEONS

A pinch of each of the following:
    pepper, lovage, fresh coriander,
    mint, dried onion
100 g (4 oz) stoned dates
1 egg yolk
15 ml (1 tbls) wine
15 ml (1 tbls) vinegar
15 ml (1 tbls) olive oil
15 ml (1 tbls) honey
5 ml (1 tsp) anchovy essence

Pound the pepper, herbs and onion together in a mortar. Add the dates and egg yolk and pound until smooth. Mix the remaining ingredients in a pan, add the mixture from the mortar, and heat gently until the sauce thickens, stirring all the time. Pour over roast pigeons and serve.

BOILED PARTRIDGE

1 partridge
a pinch of each of the following:
    pepper, lovage, celery seeds, mint,
    myrtle berries or raisins
15 ml (1 tbls) wine
15 ml (1 tbls) vinegar
15 ml (1 tbls) olive oil
5 ml (1 tsp) anchovy essence
5 ml (1 tsp) honey

Place the partridge with its feathers on in a large saucepan. Cover with cold water and simmer gently for about 45 minutes over a low heat. Pluck the bird when cooled but still wet. A freshly killed partridge may be plucked first and then braised in the sauce so that it does not get too tough. To make the sauce: pound together the pepper, lovage, celery seeds, mint, myrtle berries or raisins in a mortar, and then mix them with the wine, vinegar, olive oil, anchovy essence and honey. This makes a pleasant cold dressing to serve with the cooled partridge.

WHITE MICE
(not real mice!)

6 hard-boiled eggs
12 blanched almonds
chives
cloves or peppercorns
For the sauce:
2.5 ml (^{1}/$_2$ tsp) ground pepper
1 ml (^{1}/$_4$ tsp) cumin
pinch of caraway seeds
small bay leaf
fresh herbs to taste
50 g (2 oz) dates, finely chopped
60 ml (4 tbls) wine vinegar
60 ml (4 tbls) vegetable stock
10 ml (2 tsps) olive oil

Grind the pepper, caraway, cumin
and bay leaf together in a mortar.
Add the green herbs tied in a muslin
bag, finely chopped dates, vinegar,
wine, stock and olive oil. Bring to
a boil, then simmer gently for 20
minutes to reduce. Remove herb bag.
Cut the hard-boiled eggs in half
lengthways and place side by side on
a serving plate. Place sliced almonds
as 'ears', cloves or peppercorns as
'eyes' and use the chives as 'tails'.
Pour over the sauce and serve.
**Note: Make sure you do not eat
the 'eyes'.**

SAUCE FOR
SOFT-BOILED EGGS

100 g (4 oz) shelled pine kernels
a pinch of pepper
a pinch of lovage
15 ml (1 tbls) honey
15 ml (1 tbls) vinegar

Soak the pine kernels and let them
dry. Pound the pepper, lovage and
pine kernels in a mortar until
smooth. Mix with honey and
vinegar, and pour this sauce over
freshly boiled eggs which have been
removed from their shells.

LENTILS WITH
CHESTNUTS

100 g (4 oz) lentils
100g (4 oz) shelled chestnuts
2.5 ml (^{1}/$_2$ tsp) bicarbonate of soda
a pinch of each of the following:
    pepper, cumin, coriander seeds,
    mint, rue, pennyroyal
1 drop *asafoetida* essence
5 ml (1 tsp) anchovy essence
15 ml (1 tbls) vinegar
15 ml (1 tbls) honey
15 ml (1 tbls) olive oil

Cover the lentils with water and
simmer gently for 30 minutes. Put
the chestnuts in another pan, cover
with water, add bicarbonate of soda
and bring to the boil. Cook until
tender. Pound the pepper, cumin,
coriander seeds, mint, rue and
pennyroyal in a mortar. Moisten
with *asafoetida* essence, anchovy
essence, vinegar and honey, and pour
over the cooked chestnuts. Add olive
oil and bring to the boil, stirring all
the time. Mix with the lentils. Taste
and adjust flavouring if necessary.
Serve hot.

PEAS À LA VITELLIUS

700 g (1½ lb) dried peas, soaked
   overnight
a pinch of each of the following:
   pepper, lovage, ginger
yolks of 2 hard-boiled eggs
45 ml (3 tbls) honey
5 ml (1 tsp) anchovy essence
15 ml (1 tbls) wine
15 ml (1 tbls) vinegar
15 ml (1 tbls) olive oil

Boil the peas for about 1½ hours until
very soft. Stir to make a smooth
mixture. Pound the pepper, lovage and
ginger in a mortar and mix with the
hard-boiled egg yolks, honey, anchovy
essence, wine and vinegar. Put the
pounded mixture in a saucepan, add
the olive oil and bring to the boil.
Add to the peas, stirring until smooth
and heated through, then serve.

PEPPERED
SWEET CAKE

225 g (8 oz) spelt wheat flour
5 ml (1 tsp) baking powder
2.5 ml (½ tsp) ground rosemary
50 g (2 oz) almonds, chopped
5 ml (1 tsp) cinnamon
45 ml (3 tbls) sweet sherry
45 ml (3 tbls) grape juice
1 tbls honey
milk
To garnish:
filberts or hazelnuts

Mix the flour and baking powder.
Blend with rosemary, almonds and
cinnamon. Combine the wine, grape
juice and honey in a jug. Mix with
the dry ingredients, adding enough
milk to make a soft dropping
consistency. Bake in a 25 cm (9 in)
tin at gas mark 5, 190°C (375°F)
for approximately 30 minutes.

For a richer cake, spread the

cooked cake with liquid honey and
decorate with the nuts. Prick the
surface with a fork and drizzle a few
tablespoons of wine into the cake.

When this cake became stale the
Romans soaked it in milk and fried
it in olive oil. It was then served with
yet more honey.

TRUFFLES

12 large truffles
salt
15 ml (1 tbls) olive oil
5 ml (1 tsp) anchovy essence
15 ml (1 tbls) wine
15 ml (1 tbls) *caroenum*
15 ml (1 tbls) honey
a pinch of pepper
10 ml (2 tsps) cornflour

Scrape the truffles and put in a
saucepan with some water. Boil until
just tender, sprinkle with salt and
thread on to skewers. Grill lightly.
Put the oil, anchovy essence, wine,
caroenum, honey and pepper in a
saucepan and bring to the boil. Add
the cornflour mixed with a little
water and stir until thickened.
Remove the truffles from skewers
and serve with the sauce.

MEDIEVAL RECIPES

BEEF OR MUTTON OLIVES

Alows de beef or de motoun: 'Take fayre Bef of the quyschons, and mouton of the bottes, and kytte in the maner of Stekys; then take raw Percely, and Oynonys smal y-scredde, and yolkys of Eyroun sothe hard, and Marow or swette, and hew alle thes to-geder smal; then caste ther-on poudere of Gyngere and Saffroun, and tolle hem to-gederys with thin hond, and lay hem on the Stekys al a-brode, and caste Salt ther-to; then rolle to-gederys, and putte hem roste hem til they ben y-now; than ley hem in a dyssche, and pore ther-on Vynegre and a lityl verious, and pouder Pepir ther-on y-now, and Gyngere, and Canelle, and a fewe yolkys of hard Eyroun y-kremyd ther-on; and serue forth.'

Today, use lamb instead of mutton, and a little extra cider vinegar instead of verjuice (sour grape or apple juice). If you wish, brush the olives with beaten egg shortly before the end of the cooking time. This was called endoring, and was often done to give spit-roasted meats a golden colour.

4 thin slices of beef topside or lamb rump
1 large onion
6 hard-boiled egg yolks
15 ml (1 tbls) shredded suet
10 ml (2 tsps) finely chopped parsley
a pinch of ground ginger

a pinch of powdered saffron
salt
a little butter
cider vinegar for sprinkling
a little ground ginger, cinnamon and black pepper mixed, for sprinkling

Beat the meat thin and flat with a cutlet bat. Chop the onion finely with 4 egg yolks. Add the suet, parsley, ginger, saffron and salt to taste. Knead and squeeze until pasty, using the onion liquid to bind. (If necessary, add a few drops of water or a little extra parsley.) Spread the stuffing on the meat slices and roll them up like small Swiss rolls. Secure with wooden toothpicks. Lay side by side in a greased baking tin, with the cut edges underneath. Dot with butter. Bake, turning once, at gas mark 4, 180° C (350° F) for 35-40 minutes. Baste once or twice while baking.

Lay the olives on a warmed serving dish. Just before serving, sprinkle with vinegar and spices, and garnish with the remaining egg yolks, crumbled.

Harleian MS 279

BEEF AND VEGETABLE POTTAGE

Pottage was everyone's fare, at feasts and everyday meals alike. This one was called 'lange wortys de chare'.

900 g (2 lb) shin of beef
4–6 short pieces of marrow-bone
2.3 l (4 pt) water
2 leeks
2 sticks celery
2 onions
1/4 firm white cabbage
100 g (4 oz) 'white' breadcrumbs
a few saffron strands
10 ml (2 tsps) salt
ground black pepper

Cut the meat into 5 cm (2 in) cubes. Put in a stewpan with the bones and water. Bring to the boil and skim well. Reduce the heat, and simmer, uncovered, for about 2–2 1/2 hours. Meanwhile, prepare the vegetables and boil in a separate pan, whole or in large pieces, for 10 minutes. Drain and cut into thick slices. When the beef is just about ready, remove the marrow-bones and add the vegetables. Continue simmering until the vegetables are soft. Stir in the bread crumbs, saffron and plenty of seasoning. Bring back to the boil, and cook for 2–3 minutes. Skim off any excess fat before serving.

Harleian MS 279

The old recipe specifies a loaf of white bread which would have been a small, bun-like loaf made with unbleached soft wheat. A large scone round made with unbleached (or a mixture of white and wholemeal flour) would be something like it.

GRAPE-STUFFED BOILED CHICKEN

Chykens in hocchee: 'Take chykens and scald them, take parsel and sawge, with any other erbes, take garlec and grapes, and stoppe the chickens ful, and seeth them in good broth, so that they may esely be boyled thereinne. Messe them and cast thereto powdor-douce.'

2 chickens, each 1.1 kg (2 1/2 lb)
225 g (8 oz) green grapes
minced parsley and fresh sage leaves, mixed, to coat grapes
4 garlic cloves or to taste
salt and ground black pepper
850 ml (1 1/2 pt) chicken stock
powdor douce for sprinkling (see note)

Prepare the birds for boiling. Halve and seed the grapes, and coat them thickly with the minced herbs. Chop the garlic finely or crush it, and mix with the grapes. Season the mixture to taste, then stuff the birds with it. Truss the birds, enclosing the stuffing securely. Place the birds on a thick cloth in a stewpan. Add enough stock to come three-quarters of the way up their sides. Bring slowly to the boil, lower the heat and simmer for about 45-60 minutes until tender. Place on a warmed serving dish and sprinkle with the powdor douce.

Mrs Groundes-Peaces's Old Cookery Notebook

For the powdor douce in this case, mix 2.5 ml (1/2 tsp) each of ground cinnamon, grated nutmeg and ground black pepper, and 5 ml (1 tsp) white sugar. Recipes varied, but always included either cinnamon or ginger.

DRESSED SWAN OR PEACOCK

The flesh of both birds was thought tough and indigestible from early times. However, one or the other was served in full plumage at most great banquets because it was so handsome. Probably, as today, a cured skin with feathers, feathered head with beak and a bunch of tail features were kept for dressing a bird each time it was needed. The bird was presented as if sitting on its nest, the head being held erect by a rod or skewer thrust through the mouth, down the throat into the breast. The swan was the most expensive (it cost 3s 4d in 1380). It was presented garlanded and crowned, on a silver or gold stand, with its wings erect, neck arched backwards, head erect, at least at royal banquets. It was much more commonly served than peacock, and is occasionally still served today. Both the Vintners' Company and the Dyers' Company hold swan-upping dinners.

Swan dight: 'Kutte a Swan in the rove of the mouthe toward the brayne enlonge, and lete him blede, and kepe the blode for chawdewyn;* or elles knytte a knot on his nek, and so late his nekke breke; then skald him. Drawe him and rost him even as thou doest goce in all pyntes, and serue him forth with chawd-wyne.'

Chaudron (chawdron) was a special sauce for swans. It was made of the bird's own guts, cut small and boiled in broth with its blood and vinegar and strong spices. It looked blackish and was served hot. (Swan was quite often served as an ordinary dish, without the head.)

Pecok dight: 'Take a Pecok, breke his necke, and kutte his throte, And fle him, the skyn and the ffethurs togidre, and the hede still to the skyn of the nekke, And kepe the skyn and the ffethurs hole togiders; draw him as an hen, and kepe the bone to the necke hole, And roste him, and set the bone of the necke aboue the broche, as he was wonte to sitte a lyve, And aboue the legges to the body, as he was wonte to sitte a-lyve; And whan he is rosted ynowe, take him of, And lete him kele; And then wynde the skyn with the fethurs and the taile aboughte the body, And serue him forthe as he were a-live; or elles pull him dry, And roste him and serue him as thou doest a henne.'

In other words, truss in an erect position after flaying; roast, cool, then cover the skin and feathers like a jacket. Present like a swan, but with gilded comb instead of a crown, and a gold chain instead of a garland.

Harleian MS 4016

HOT WINE BEVERAGE

A caudle was a hot wine drink thickened with eggs, which was drunk at breakfast or bedtime. This was a version for Lent or Fridays when, strictly, eggs were not allowed.

275 ml (1/2 pt) water
850 ml (11/2 pt) white wine
225 g (8 oz) ground almonds
2.5 ml (1/2 tsp) ground ginger
5 ml (1 tsp) clear honey or white sugar
a good pinch of salt
a good pinch of powdered saffron or a few drops of yellow food colouring

Bring the water and wine to the boil in a saucepan. Tip in the almonds, and add the ginger, honey or sugar and salt. Stir in the saffron or food colouring, and leave off the heat to steep for 15-30 minutes. Bring back to the boil, and serve very hot, in small heatproof bowls.

The Forme of Cury

ALMOND MILK

'Cold milk of almondes' was a basic ingredient used as a fast-day substitute for other thickened liquids in many medieval dishes. Only one recipe is known, dated about 1467. Modern ground almonds make a slightly gritty liquid; grinding in a blender before use helps, but do not let them 'oil'. Use the following proportions:

50 g (2 oz) almonds, blanched, skinned and ground
For thin milk:
2.5 ml (1/2 tsp) honey or white sugar

a good pinch of salt
200 ml (7 fl oz) boiling water
30 ml (2 tbls) white wine
For thick milk (like coating white sauce):
1.5 ml (1/4 tsp) honey or white sugar
a good pinch of salt
65 ml (21/2 fl oz) boiling water
15 ml (1 tbls) white wine

Put the almonds in a bowl. Add the honey or sugar and salt to the water, and pour over the almonds. Leave to stand for 15–30 minutes, stirring occasionally. Mix in the wine. Strain thin milk if a particular recipe requires it. Refrigerate in a covered container for up to 48 hours.

The original recipe suggests boiling the water with the sweetening and salt, one suspects to a syrup – indicating that the medieval palate liked its sauces sweetened much more heavily than above. Add extra honey or sugar to dessert dishes.

COOKING SUNDRY FISH

Floundres boiled: 'Take floundres and drawe hem in the side by the hede [gut through a slit below the head] . . . and make sauce of water and salt and a good quantite of ale; and whan hit biginneth to boile, skeme it, and caste hem there-to; And late hem sethe [boil]; and serue hem forth hote; and no sauce but salt, or as a man luste.'

Shrympes: 'Take shrympes, and seth hem in water and a litull salt, and lete hem boil ones or a litull more. And serue hem forthe colde; And no maner sauce but vinegre.'

Sole, boiled . . . or fryed: 'Take a sole and do away the hede, and drawe him as a plais [plaice – or flounder, see above] and fle [skin] him; and make sauce of water, parcelly and salt; And whan hit bygynneth to boile, skeme it clene, and lete boyle ynogh. And if thoy wilt haue him in sauce, take hime whan he is y-sodde [add it after boiling] . . . Or elles take a sole, and do away the hede; draw him, and scalde him, and pryk him with

a knyfe in diuerse [various] place for brekyng of the skin [to prevent curling]; And fry it in oyle, or elles in pured [clarified] buttur.'

Follow modern cooking methods, i.e. simmer or poach the fish, rather than boiling furiously. There is no need to skim impurities off modern salt, tap-water and beer.

Harleian MS 4016

SAUCE VERT

'Take percely, myntes, diteyne, peletre, a foil or ij of cost marye, a cloue of garleke. And take faire brede, and stepe it with vynegre and piper, and salt; and grynde al this to-gedre, and tempre it up with wynegre, or with eisel, and serue it forth.'

This was a very popular type of sauce in medieval times because it masked the taste of fish which was slightly 'off', over-salted or just muddy. Mint sauce is almost the only modern survivor. Dittany, pellitory, and costmary had almost gone out of favour by the end of Tudor times, when more pleasing herbs had come into use. Use any fresh herbs you can get, the more the better.

Suggested proportions:
Leaves of 10–12 sprigs parsley, mint and other fresh herbs
1 garlic clove
50 g (2 oz) fine 'white' breadcrumbs
30 ml (2 tbls) cider vinegar
salt
freshly ground black pepper
wine vinegar and/or water as needed

Chop the herbs finely. Parsley and mint should predominate. Squeeze the garlic over the herbs in a mortar. Sprinkle the breadcrumbs with the cider vinegar and leave for 10 minutes. Add to the herbs with salt and pepper. Pound until well blended. Then add enough wine vinegar or water, or a mixture, to give you a consistency rather like thickened mint sauce (or green bread sauce). Serve with broiled or poached fish.

Ashmole MS 1439

SWEET CHEESE FLAN

Tart de bry: 'Take a croste ynch depe in trape. Take zolkes of ayren rawe and chese ruayn. Medle it and zolkes togyd and do ther-to poudor, gynger, sugar, saffron and salt. Do it in a trape, bak it and serve it forth.'

The costly medieval sugar came in close-packed loaves, whitish outside with treacly residues in the centre. The wealthy had whitish sugar cut or scraped off the loaf but in coarser grains than granulated sugar. Caster sugar is recommended, however, for a lighter cheesecake.

'Chese ruayn' meant any rich soft cheese. Brie was well known in England but must have been costly.

Shortcrust pastry made with
   150 g (5 oz) flour and 65 g
   (2½ oz) lard
a pinch of powdered saffron
15 ml (1 tbls) very hot water
350 g (12 oz) Brie cheese, without
   rind, or full fat soft cheese
4 egg yolks
50 g (2 oz) caster sugar
a good pinch of ground ginger
a pinch of salt

Use the pastry to line an 20 cm (8 in) flan case. Steep the saffron powder in the water until the liquid is deep gold. Meanwhile, beat the cheese until creamy and quite smooth. In a separate bowl, beat the egg yolks and sugar together until thick and pale. Beat in the softened cheese little by little, then the ginger, salt and saffron water. Turn the mixture into the prepared case. Bake at gas mark 5, 190° C (375° F) for 20–25 minutes or until just set in the centre. Serve warm or cold the same day.

The Forme of Cury

PEARS IN WINE SYRUP

This is one of the earliest of many recipes for 'warduns in syruppe'. It suggests mulberries as red fruit, but loganberries make a good modern substitute. It also suggests 'wyn crete or vernage' for the syrup; this usually meant a sweet southern Italian or Cypriot white wine or one from Tuscany. Wardens were a large type of pear.

3 large firm dessert pears
298 g (10 oz) can mulberries or
    loganberries
275 ml (½ pt) full-flavoured red
    wine
a few drops of red food colouring
150 ml (¼ pt) sweet white Italian
    wine
25 g (1 oz) white sugar
a good pinch of ground ginger
a small pinch of cinnamon
a small pinch of ground black pepper

Peel the pears but leave them whole. Gouge out the hard cores from the round end if you wish. Drain the berries. Put the pears and berries in a saucepan, and pour the red wine over them with a few drops of colouring. Simmer the fruit until the pears are tender, turning them often to colour them pink evenly. Cool in the liquid, turning them from time to time to deepen the colour. Drain, reserving the liquid. Cut the pears into halves or into quarters if you wish. Sieve the soft fruit and return to the pan with the cooking liquid. Put the white wine, sugar and spices in a clean pan. Boil to 105° C (215° F) or until you have a fairly thick syrup which will glaze the fruit. Add the pears, bring back to the boil, and cook for 2–3 minutes. Serve hot, with the warmed sieved fruit and red wine as a sauce.

Ancient Cookery

The original recipe specifies powdor douce to flavour the syrup. The sugar, ginger and cinnamon mixture is here based on a Tudor recipe which used 50 g (2 oz) sugar, 7 g (¼ oz) ginger and 3.5 g (⅛ oz) cinnamon.

GINGERBREAD

'Take goode honey & clarifie it on the fere, & take fayre paynemayn or wastel brede & grate it, & caste it into the boylenge hony, & stere it will togydr faste with a sklse that bren not to the vessell. & thanne take it doun and put thein ginger, long pepere & saundres, & tempere it up with thin handel; & than put hem to a flatt boyste & strawe theron suger, & pick therin clowes round about by the egge and in the myudes yf it plece you &c.'

575 ml (1 pint) honey
435 g (15 oz) breadcrumbs
25 ml (5 tsp) ground ginger
5 ml (1 tsp) pepper
5 ml (1 tsp) ground sandalwood
cloves

Place honey in a small saucepan and bring to the boil on a low heat. Skim off the scum that forms on the top of the honey. Stir in the breadcrumbs then remove from the heat. Mix in the spices and place the mixture in a Swiss roll tin. Cut into pieces when cold and serve decorated with whole cloves (optional).

Harleian MS 4016

MUTTON IN BEER

To Stewe Stekes of Mutton: Take a legge of mutton and cot it in small slices, and put it in a chafer, and put therto a pottell of ale, and scome it cleane then putte therto seven or eyghte onions thyn slyced, and after they have boyled one hour, putte ther-to a dyshe of swete butter, and so lette them boyle tyll they be tender, and then put therto a lyttel peper and salte.

900 g (2 lb) leg of lamb or mutton
575 ml (1 pint) brown ale
1 large or 2 small onions, thinly sliced
5 ml (1 tsp) salt
pepper to taste
25 g (1 oz) butter
bread slices, cut into crustless cubes, to serve

Bone the meat, trim off the skin and excess fat, and cut into thin slices across the grain. Place in a heavy pan with the beer and onions, cover and simmer for an hour before adding the salt, pepper and butter. Simmer for a further 20–30 minutes until tender. Serve on cubes of crustless bread in a deep dish.

A Proper Newe Book of Cokerye

Stewed steaks later developed into 'Scotch collops', one of the most popular dishes of the 17th and 18th centuries.

REAL MINCE PIE

For Pyes of Mutton or Beefe: Shred your meat and Suet togither fine, season it with cloves, mace, Pepper, and some Saffron, great Raisins, Corance and prunes, and so put it into your Pyes.

700 g (1¼ lbs) lean mutton or beef
100 g (4 oz) suet
2.5 ml (½ tsp) ground cloves
5 ml (1 tsp) ground mace
2.5 ml (½ tsp) black pepper
a pinch of saffron
50 g (2 oz) raisins
50 g (2 oz) currants
50 g (2 oz) stoned prunes, chopped

For the pastry:
450 g (1 lb) plain flour
10 ml (2 tsps) salt
100 g (4 oz) lard
150 ml (¼ pt) water
60 ml (4 tbls) milk
For the glaze:
15 ml (1 tbls) each of butter, sugar and rosewater melted together

Mince the meat, and mix in the suet, spices, pepper, saffron and dried fruit. To make the pastry, sift the flour and salt together into a large mixing bowl and make a well in the centre. Heat the lard, water and milk until boiling and pour into the well. Quickly beat the mixture together with a spoon to form a soft dough, and knead until smooth on a lightly floured board. Cut off a quarter of

the pastry, and keep covered until required to make the lid. Mould the larger piece of pastry to form the base and sides of the pie within a 20 cm (8 in) diameter, 5 cm (2 in) deep loose-bottomed tin. Pack the meat into the pie and dampen the edges of the pie wall. Roll out the remaining pastry to make a lid and firmly press into place. Trim the edges, using the surplus pastry for decoration, and cut a hole in the centre of the lid. Bake in the centre of the oven at gas mark 7, 220°C (425°F) for 15 minutes, then reduce the temperature to gas mark 4, 180°C (350°F) for a further 1¼ hours. Remove the sides of the tin, brush with the glaze, and return to the oven for a further 15 minutes. Serve cold.

A.W.: A Book of Cookrye Very necessary for all such as delight therin

This pie, with its combination of meat, suet and dried fruit, is the predecessor of today's 'mince pies', in which the meat has been totally replaced by the fruit. It still makes an excellent dish for Christmastime, providing a substantial and finely flavoured dish for a buffet supper.

SWEET CHICKEN PÂTÉ

To make a mortis: Take almonds and blanche them, and beat them in a morter, and boyle a Chicken, and take al the flesh of him, and beate it, and straine them together, with milke and water, and so put them into a pot, and put in Suger, and stirre them still, and when it hath boyled a good while, take it of, and set it a cooling in a payle of water, and straine it againe with Rose water into a dish.

½ chicken
50 g (2 oz) blanched almonds
150 ml (¼ pt) milk
15 ml (1 tbls) sugar
15 ml (1 tbls) rosewater

Put the chicken in a saucepan, cover with water and boil until tender – about 45 minutes. Drain, and pick all the meat from the bones. While the chicken is boiling, use either a mortar and pestle or a blender to grind the almonds and milk together to form a smooth paste. Grind the cooked chicken into this paste, then place the mixture in a saucepan with the sugar and cook over a gentle heat for 10–15 minutes, stirring continuously. Cool the saucepan in a bowl of cold water, beat in the rosewater, and finally fork the resulting pâté either down into a deep bowl, or into a symmetrical shape on a plate ready for the table.

Thomas Dawson:
The good huswifes Jewell, pt. 1

This 'mortrews', a survival of the medieval standing pottages, makes a pleasant and interesting addition to any buffet or summer salad.

EGGS IN MUSTARD SAUCE

Sodde Egges: Seeth your Egges almost harde, then peele them and cut them in quarters, then take a little butter in a frying panne and melt it a little broune, then put to it in to the panne, a little Vinegar, Mustarde, Pepper and Salte, and then put it into a platter upon your Egges.

For each egg take:
25 g (1 oz) butter
5 ml (1 tsp) made mustard
5 ml (1 tsp) vinegar
a pinch of salt
pepper to taste

Boil the eggs for 5 minutes. Meanwhile, lightly brown the butter in a small pan and allow it to cool a little before quickly stirring in the remaining ingredients. When the eggs are ready, peel and quarter them on a warm dish. Reheat the sauce, and pour it over the eggs immediately before serving.

J. Partridge: *The Widowes Treasure*

THICK PEA POTTAGE

To boyle yong Peason or Beanes: First shale them and seethe them in faire water, then take them out of the water and put them into boyling milk, then take the yolks of Egs with crums of bread, and ginger, and straine them thorow a strainer with the said milk, then take chopped percely, Saffron and Salt, and serve it foorth for Pottage.

25 g (1 oz) fresh breadcrumbs
1 egg yolk
5 ml (1 tsp) chopped parsley
5 ml (1 tsp) salt
2.5 ml ($^{1}/_{2}$ tsp) ground ginger
a pinch of saffron

275 ml ($^{1}/_{2}$ pt) milk
350 g (12 oz) cooked peas, or
    525 g (19 oz) can of peas

Beat together the breadcrumbs, egg yolk, parsley, salt, ginger and saffron. Bring the milk almost to the boil, pour in the peas and the breadcrumb mixture, then bring to the boil over a low heat, stirring continuously. This thick pottage can be used as a quickly made and very substantial warming soup, or it may be served as a vegetable, making an excellent accompaniment to fish dishes.

A.W. : *A Book of Cookrye Very necessary for all such as delight therin*

PRUNE TART

To make a Tarte of Prunes: Take Prunes and wash them, then boil them with faire water, cut in halfe a peny loaf of white bread, and take them out and strain them with Claret wine, season it with sinamon, Ginger and Sugar, and a little Rosewater, make the paste as fine as you can, and dry it, and fill it, and let it drie in the oven, take it out and cast on it Biskets and Carawaies.

350 g (12 oz) prunes
100 g (4 oz) fresh white breadcrumbs
275 ml ($^1/_2$ pt) red wine
5 ml (1 tsp) cinnamon
5 ml (1 tsp) ground ginger
100 g (4 oz) sugar
15 ml (1 tbls) rosewater
For the pastry:
75 g (3 oz) butter
100 g (4 oz) plain flour
5 ml (1 tsp) caster sugar
1 egg, beaten

Soak the prunes overnight, then simmer in a little water for 10–15 minutes until tender. To make the pastry, rub the butter into the flour, mix in the sugar, and slowly stir in the eggs until it forms a soft dough which can be lightly kneaded with the hands. Roll out the pastry, and use it to line a 20 cm (8 in) diameter, 5 cm (2 in) deep flan ring. Line the pastry with greaseproof paper, fill with uncooked haricot beans or crusts, and bake blind at gas mark 7, 220°C (425°F) for 15 minutes. Remove the beans and greaseproof paper. To make the filling, drain and stone the prunes, then blend them with the remaining ingredients to form a smooth thick paste. Spoon the filling into the pastry case, and return to the oven to bake at gas mark 4, 180°C (350°F) for 1$^1/_2$ hours. Serve either hot or cold.

A.W. : *A Book of Cookrye Very necessary for all such as delight therin*

PRUNES IN SYRUP

To make Prunes in sirrope: Take Prunes, and put Claret wine to them, and Sugar, as much as you think will make them pleasant, let all these seeth together till yee thinke the liquor looke like a sirrope, and that your Prunes be well swollen: and so keepe them in a vessell as yee doe greene Ginger.

225 g (8 oz) prunes
425 ml ($^3/_4$ pt) claret
100 g (4 oz) sugar

Soak the prunes overnight in the claret, then simmer the prunes, claret and sugar for 10-15 minutes until the prunes are fully swollen and tender. They may then be eaten directly, or sealed into sterilised jars for use at a future time.

J. Partridge: *The Treasurie of Commodious Conceites and Hidden Secrets*

This rich but simple dish provides a convenient example of the 'suckets' eaten with a fork during the banquet course.

POACHED PEARS

To conserve wardens all the yeere in sirrop: Take your wardens and put them into a great Earthen pot, and cover them close, set them in an Oven when you have set in your white bread, & when you have drawne your white bread, and your pot, & that they be so colde as you may handle them, then pill the thin skinne from them over a pewter dish, that you may save all the sirroppe that falleth from them: put to them a quarte of the same sirrope, and a pinte of Rosewater, and boile them together with a fewe Cloves and Sinnamon, and when it is reasonable thick and cold, put your wardens and Sirroppe into a Galley pot and see alwaies that the Syrrop bee above the Wardens, or any other thing that you conserve.

1.3 kg (3 lb) pears
850 ml (1½ pt) water
225 g (8 oz) sugar
150 ml (¼ pt) rosewater
5 ml (1 tsp) whole cloves
2 sticks cinnamon

Place the pears in a casserole and bake at gas mark 4, 180°C (350°F) for 1-1½ hours until soft to the touch. Cool, then peel. Simmer any liquor which runs from them with a syrup made from the remaining ingredients, add the pears, and simmer for a few minutes before cooling.

Thomas Dawson:
The good huswifes Jewell, pt. 2

JUMBLES OR KNOTTED BISCUITS

To make Iombils a hundred: Take twenty Egges and put them into a pot both the yolkes & the white, beat them wel, then take a pound of beaten suger and put to them, and stirre them wel together, then put to it a quarter of a peck of flower, and make a hard paste thereof, and then with Anniseeds moulde it well, ane make it in little rowles beeing long, and tye them in knots, and wet the ends in Rosewater, then put them into a pan of seething water, but even in one waum, then take them out with a Skimmer and lay them in a cloth to drie, this being don lay them in a tart panne, the bottome beeing oyled, then put them into a temperat Oven for one howre, turning them often in the Oven.

2 eggs
100 g (4 oz) sugar
15 ml (1 tbls) aniseed or caraway
175 g (6 oz) plain flour

Beat the eggs in a large basin, then beat in the sugar, the aniseed or caraway, and finally the flour, thus forming a stiff dough. Knead the dough on a lightly floured board, and form into rolls approximately 1 cm (³/₈ in) in diameter by 10 cm (4 in) in length. Tie each of these in a simple knot and plunge them, five or six at a time, into a pan of boiling water, where they will immediately sink to the bottom. After a short time dislodge the knots from the bottom of the pan with a spoon so that they float and swell for a minute or two. Then lift the knots out with a perforated spoon, and allow them to drain on a clean tea-towel laid over a wire rack. Arrange the knots on lightly buttered baking sheets and bake for 15 minutes at gas mark 4, 180°C (350°F), then turn the knots over and return to the oven for 10–15 minutes until golden.

Thomas Dawson:
The good huswifes Jewell, pt. 2

SWEET CUBES OF JELLIED MILK

A white leach: Take a quart of newe milke, and three ounces weight of Isinglasse, half a pounde of beaten suger, and stirre them together, and let it boile half a quarter of an hower till it be thicke, stirring them al the while: then straine it with three sponfull of Rosewater, then put it into a platter and let it coole, and cut it in squares. Lay it faire in dishes, and lay golde upon it.

25 ml (5 tsps) **gelatine**
575 ml (1 pt) **milk**
100 g (4 oz) **sugar**
25 ml (5 tsps) **rosewater**

Sprinkle the gelatine on to 60 ml (4 tbls) of the milk in a cup. Leave for 5 minutes before standing the cup in hot water and stirring the gelatine until it is completely dissolved. Warm the remaining milk, stir in the gelatine and the sugar, and simmer, stirring continuously, for 5 minutes. Remove from the heat, stir in the rosewater, and pour into a shallow baking dish about 15 cm (6 in) square which has been freshly rinsed in cold water. Allow to set firmly in a cool place before cutting into squares with a sharp knife. The squares may then be either arranged in a regular pattern or stacked as a pyramid on a flat plate ready for the table.

Thomas Dawson:
The good huswifes Jewell, pt. 2

This unusual dish has a delicious, cool sweet flavour and a translucent ivory-white appearance similar to Turkish delight.

POSSET

To make a good Possett Curde: First take the Milke and seeth it on the fire, and before it seeth put in your Egges according to the quantitye of your Milke, but see that your Egges be tempered with some of your milke that standeth on the fire, and you must stirre it still untill it seeth, and beginning to rise, then take it from the fire, and have your drinke ready in a fair Bason on a chafing dishe of coles and put your Milke in to the bason as it standeth, and cover it, and let it stand a while, then take it up, and cast on ginger and synomon.

3 eggs
575 ml (1 pt) **milk**
275 ml (¹/₂ pt) **strong brown ale**
cinnamon and ground ginger

Beat the eggs into the milk, and heat gently, stirring continuously, until the mixture has thickened and is about to rise to the boil. Meanwhile, heat the ale almost to boiling point and pour into a large warmed bowl. Quickly pour the hot egg and milk mixture into the ale from a good height, cover the bowl and leave in a warm place for 5 minutes to allow the curd to set. Sprinkle a little cinnamon and ginger over the posset, which is now ready to be served.

J. Partridge: *The Widowes Treasure*

Simple possets of this type became much richer and sweeter as they grew in popularity in the later 17th century.

SUGAR PLATES AND WINE GLASSES

To make a paste of Suger, whereof a man may make al manner of fruits, and other fine thinges with their forme, as Plates, Dishes, Cuppes, and such like thinges, wherewith you may furnish a Table. Take Gumme and dragant as much as you wil, and steep it in Rosewater till it be mollified, and for four ounces of suger take of it the bignes of a beane, the juyce of Lemons, a walnut shel ful, and a little of the white of an eg. But you must first take the gumme, and beat it so much with a pestell in a brasen morter, till it be come like water, then put in the juyce with the white of an egge, incorporating al these wel together, this don take four ounces of fine white suger well beaten to powder, and cast it into ye morter by a little and little until they be turned into ye form of paste, then take it out of the said morter, and bray it upon the powder of suger, as it were meale or flower, untill it be like soft paste, to the end you may turn it, and fashion it which way you wil. When you have brought your paste to this fourme spread it abroad upon great or smal leaves as you shall thinke it good, and so shal you form or make what things you wil, as is aforesaid, with such fine knackes as may serve a Table taking heede there stand no hotte thing nigh it. At the end of the Banket they may eat all, and break the Platters, Dishes, Glasses, Cuppes, and all other things, for this paste is very delicate and saverous.

2.5 ml ($^{1}/_{2}$ tsp) gelatine
5 ml (1 tsp) lemon juice
10 ml (2 tsps) rosewater
$^{1}/_{2}$ egg white, lightly beaten
350–450 g (12–16 oz) icing sugar

Stir the gelatine into the lemon juice and rosewater in a basin and place over a bowl of hot water until melted. Stir in the lightly beaten egg white, and work in the icing sugar, little by little, until a dough is formed. It can then be turned out on a board dusted with icing sugar, and kneaded until completely smooth. Having dusted the board with a little cornflour, the mixture is then rolled out thinly and pressed into saucers, plates, or the bowls of wine glasses to mould it into the required shapes.

The surplus trimmed from the rims may then be modelled in the form of baluster stems and bases, either for the glasses or to convert the saucers into standing tazzas for the better display of sweetmeats. A little royal icing can be used to join the various sections together after they have been allowed to dry and harden for a few hours. Glasses and dishes made in this porcelain-like translucent material can provide an interesting range of vessels for the presentation of any cold dry sweetmeats on the banqueting table. Sugar wine glasses filled with crystallised flowers make a particularly elegant display, the contrast of textures and colours bringing a rare beauty to the table.

Thomas Dawson:
The good huswifes Jewell, pt. 2

STUART RECIPES

DIET BREAD

The receypte of the Dyett bread:
Take halfe a pecke of fyne
Wheaten Flower, three handfull
of sage shredd small, An ounce
and a halfe of ordinary Fennell
seede lightly bruised, strawe the
sage and the Fennell seede amongst
the Flower, and so with barme
kneade and bake ytt as you do
other breade, and eate ytt nott
until ytt be a day old.

400 g (14 oz) plain flour
30 ml (2 tbls) dried sage
15 g (½ oz) fennel seed, bruised
15 g (½ oz) dried yeast mixed with 5
   ml (1 tsp) sugar and
   275 ml (½ pt) warm water

Mix the dry ingredients in a warm
bowl, make a well in the centre and
work in the liquid. Knead, and then
leave to rise in a warm place for
1 hour. Knead the dough on a
floured board, shape into a round
cob or a number of small cakes, and
allow to prove for 15 minutes before
baking at gas mark 8, 230°C (450°F)
for 15 minutes, and then for a
further 40 minutes at gas mark 6,
200°C (400°F). This bread has a
delicate aniseed flavour, and makes
an interesting accompaniment to
soups, fish or cheese.

A Temple Newsam recipe quoted in
The Gentlewoman's Kitchen

DUTCH PUDDING

Take a pound and a halfe of Fresh
Beef, all lean, take a pound and a
quarter of Beef Suet, sliced both
very small, then take a halfpenny
stale Loaf and grate it, a handfull
of Sage and a little Winter Savory,
a little Time, shred these very
small; take four Eggs, half a pint
of Cream, a few Cloves, Nutmegs,
Mace and Pepper, finely beaten,
mingle them all together very well,
with a little Salt; roll it all up
together in a green Colwort Leaf,
and then tye it up hard in a
Linnen-Cloth, garnish your Dish
with grated bread and serve it up
with mustard in Sawcers.

350 g (12 oz) coarsely minced lean beef
225 g (8 oz) suet
100 g (4 oz) dry breadcrumbs
10 ml (2 tsps) dried sage
5 ml (1 tsp) dried savory
5 ml (1 tsp) dried thyme
2 eggs
1.5 ml (¼ tsp) ground cloves
1.5 ml (¼ tsp) grated nutmeg
1.5 ml (¼ tsp) ground mace
1.5 ml (¼ tsp) pepper
10 ml (2 tsps) salt
1–2 large cabbage leaves
To serve:
fresh breadcrumbs
freshly made English mustard

Mix all the ingredients together and
form into a round ball. Wrap in a large
cabbage leaf or 2 smaller ones, and tie
up tightly in a linen cloth. Plunge into
boiling water and simmer for 2 hours.
To serve, turn out of the cloth on to a
bed of fresh breadcrumbs, accompanied
by a saucer of English mustard. The
dish looks just like a cabbage at this
stage, but may be carved with ease.

Elizabeth Cromwell: *The Court and Kitchen of*
Mrs Elizabeth Commonly called Joan Cromwell

This dish is delicious served with a
fruit sauce made from blackberries.

SCOTCH COLLOPS

*To Make Scotch Collops: R. a
legge of Mutton, cutt itt in round
pieces as broad as you can, & the
thickness of a thin halfe-crowne,
fry them in sweet butter very
browne, but not too hard, then
take four or five spoonfull of
vinegar, an onion slit, halfe a
nuttmegge grated, Lemon-pill, an
Anchovee, a little horseradish, &
oysters if you have them, putt all
into the Frying-pan together with
the meat, & a quarter of a pound
of butter beaten thick, tosse them
in the Pan a while over the fire,
but do not let them boyle, then
heat your dish, rubb it with
Shallot or garlick, & send them
upp quick.*

450 g (1 lb) lean lamb or mutton
175 g (6 oz) butter
75 ml (5 tbls) claret
30 ml (2 tbls) vinegar
1 onion
2 anchovy fillets
15 ml (1 tbls) horseradish sauce
1 garlic clove

Thinly slice the meat, and stir fry
gently with half the butter for 5–10
minutes until browned. Remove
from the heat, and add all the
remaining ingredients, except for the
garlic. Heat gently for a few minutes,
stirring the pan continuously, until
almost at boiling point. Slice the
garlic, and rub it around the inside
of the serving dish before pouring in
the collops. Serve immediately. This
is an excellent way of making a rich
and full-flavoured meat dish in a
very short time.

The Savile Recipe Book, 1683, quoted in
The Gentlewoman's Kitchen

CHICKEN CULLIS

*To make a cullis as white as
snowe and in the nature of gelly:
Take a cocke, scalde, wash and
draw him clene, seeth it in white
wine or rhenish wine, skum it
cleane, clarifie the broth after it is
strained, then take a pinte of thicke
& sweet creame, straine that to
your clarified broth, and your
broth will become exceeding faire
and white; then take powdred
ginger, fine white sugar and
Rosewater, seething your cullis
when you season it, to make it
take the colour the better.*

1 chicken
850 ml (1½ pt) white wine
1 egg white, lightly beaten
575 ml (1 pt) single cream
2.5 ml (½ tsp) ground ginger
30 ml (2 tbls) sugar
15 ml (1 tbls) rosewater

Simmer the chicken in the wine until
tender – about 45–50 minutes.
Remove the chicken from the pan
and keep it hot. Beat the egg white
into the stock and continue to whisk
over a moderate heat until it comes
to the boil. Stop whisking
immediately and allow the liquid to
rise to the top of the pan before
removing it from the heat for a few
minutes to allow the fine particles to
form a soft curd with the egg white.
Pour the liquid through a fine cloth
into a clean pan, place on a gentle
heat, and stir slowly while pouring in
the cream. Heat the cullis almost to
boiling point, stirring continuously,
and finally add the ginger, sugar and
rosewater just before serving. The
cullis may be poured over the chicken
resting on crustless cubes of white
bread, in a deep dish. Alternatively, it
can be served separately as a soup.

Sir Hugh Platt: *Delightes for Ladies*

BRAWN

To bake Brawne: Take two Buttocks... take Lard, cut it in pieces as big as your little finger, and season it very well with Pepper, Cloves, Mace, Nutmeg, and Salt, put each of them into an earthen Pot, put in a pint of Claret-wine, a pound of Mutton Suet. So close it with paste, let the Oven be well heated, and so bake them...

900 g – 1.4 kg (2–3lb) joint of pork
350 ml (¹/₂ bottle) claret
50 g (2 oz) suet
10 ml (2 tsps) salt
2.5 ml (¹/₂ tsp) ground mace
1.5 ml (¹/₄ tsp) pepper
1.5 ml (¹/₄ tsp) ground cloves
1.5 ml (¹/₄ tsp) grated nutmeg
Shortcrust pastry made with:
100 g (4 oz) plain flour
50 g (2 oz) lard

Trim any fat or rind from the joint, and cut into strips. Truss the joint tightly, place in a deep casserole, then add the strips of fat and the remaining ingredients except for the pastry. Roll out the pastry, and use it to cover the casserole, carefully sealing the edges. Bake at gas mark 4, 180°C (350°F) for 2¹/₂ hours, then leave in a cool place overnight. Remove the crust, lift out the joint, wipe clean, and carve as required. The remaining stock can be used to provide a highly flavoured basis for soups etc.

Rebecca Price: The Compleat Cook

SALAD

For the salad:
young leaves of lettuce, sorrel, mustard, cress, dandelion, spinach, radishes
225 g (8 oz) capers

12 dates, sliced lengthways
50 g (2 oz) raisins
50 g (2 oz) currants
50 g (2 oz) blanched almonds
6 figs, sliced
6 mandarin oranges, peeled and divided into segments
For the decoration:
5 small branches of rosemary
4 lemons
225 g (8 oz) fresh or glacé cherries
6 hard-boiled eggs

Mix the contents of the salad together (reserving half the capers, dates, almonds and oranges for decoration) and spread evenly across a wide shallow dish. Spike each branch of rosemary into the pointed end of five half-lemons, and hang with the cherries before placing one in the centre of the salad, and the remaining four equidistant around it. Prick 4 half-eggs with the reserved almonds and dates, both sliced lengthways, and place these between the four half-lemons. Quarter the remaining eggs, and alternate with slices of lemon just within the brim of the dish. Then decorate the brim with alternating orange segments and small piles of capers.

The Second Book of Cookery

SYLLABUB

My Lady Middlesex makes Syllabubs for little Glasses with spouts, thus Take 3 pints of sweet Cream, one of quick white wine (or Rhenish), and a good wine glassful (better the ¹/₄ of a pint) of sack; mingle them with about three quarters of a pound of fine Sugar in Powder. Beat all these together with a whisk, till all appeareth converted into froth. Then pour it into your little Syllabub-glasses, and let them stand all night. The next day the curd will be thick and firm above, and the drink clear under it. I conceive it may do well, to put into each glass (when you pour your liquor into it) a sprig of Rosemary a little bruised, or a little Lemon-peel, or some such thing to quicken the taste … or Nutmegs, or Mace, or Cloves, a very little.

575 ml (1 pt) double cream
200 ml (7 fl oz) Rhenish white wine
30 ml (2 tbls) dry sherry
100 g (4 oz) caster sugar
sprigs of rosemary or the thinly
   peeled zest of a lemon

Beat the cream, wines and sugar together to form a thick froth, and spoon into large wine glasses. Insert the rosemary or lemon as desired, and allow to stand in a cool place for at least 12 hours before serving. The resulting syllabub is one of the most delicately flavoured, smooth and delicious of all 17th-century dishes.

Sir Kenelm Digby:
The Closet of Sir Kenelm Digby Opened

SACK POSSET

My Lord of Carlisle's Sack-possett: Take a Pottle of Cream, and boil in it a little whole Cinnamon, and three or four flakes of Mace. To this proportion of Cream put in eighteen yolkes of Eggs, and eight of the whites; a pint of Sack. Beat your Eggs very well, and mingle them with your Sack, Put in three quarters of a pound of Sugar into the Wine and Eggs with a Nutmeg

grated, and a little beaten Cinnamon; set the basin on the fire with the wine and Eggs, and let it be hot. Then put in the Cream boyling from the fire, pour it on high, but stir it not; cover it with a dish, and when it is settled, strew on the top a little fine Sugar mingled with three grains of Ambergreece and one grain of Musk and serve it up.

9 egg yolks
4 egg whites
275 ml (¹/₂ pt) dry sherry
1.5 ml (¹/₄ tsp) cinnamon
1.5 ml (¹/₄ tsp) ground mace
2.5 ml (¹/₂ tsp) grated nutmeg
1 l (2 pt) single cream
175 g (6 oz) sugar

Beat together the egg yolks, egg whites, sherry and spices. Place in a large saucepan and heat gently, stirring constantly, until warm but still not thickened. Heat the cream and sugar together and, as it rises to the full boil, pour from a good height into the warm eggs and sherry mixture. Allow the posset to stand in a warm place for a few minutes, sprinkle a little sugar across its surface, and serve.

Sir Kenelm Digby:
The Closet of Sir Kenelm Digby Opened

SPICE CAKE

To make an Extraordinary Good Cake: Take half a bushel of the best flour you can get, very finely searced, and lay it on a large pastry board, make a hole in the middle thereof, put to it three pounds of the best butter you can get; with 14 pounds of currants finely picked and rubbed, three quarts of good new thick cream, 2 pounds of fine sugar beaten, 3 pints of new ale barm or yeast, 4 ounces of cinnamon beaten fine and searced, also an ounce of beaten ginger, 2 ounces of nutmegs beaten fine and searced; put all these material together, and work them up to an indifferent stiff paste. Keep it warm till the oven be hot, then make it up and bake it, being baked an hour and a half ice it, then take 4 pounds of double refined sugar, beat it and searce it, and put it in a clean scowered skillet the quantity of a gallon, and boil it to a candy height with a little rosewater, then draw the cake, run it all over, and set it in the oven till it be candied.

75 g (3 oz) butter
450 g (1 lb) plain flour
350 g (12 oz) currants
50 g (2 oz) sugar
2.5 ml (1/2 tsp) ground cinnamon
2.5 ml (1/2 tsp) ground ginger
1.5 ml (1/4 tsp) grated nutmeg
275 ml (1/2 pt) cream
15 g (1/2 oz) dried yeast mixed with
    5 ml (1 tsp) sugar and
    150 ml (1/4 pt) warm water
For the glazing:
15 ml (1 tbls) sugar
15 ml (1 tbls) rosewater

Rub the butter into the flour, add the remainder of the dry ingredients, and mix in the cream and yeast to form a soft dough. Leave to rise in a warm place for about 1 hour, when it will have doubled in size, then knead and place in a greased 20 cm (8 in) cake tin. Leave to prove for 20 minutes, then bake at gas mark 7, 220°C (425°F) for 20 minutes, then for 1 hour at gas mark 5, 190°C (375°F). Melt the sugar in the rosewater over a low heat, and brush this glaze over the cake immediately after removing it from the oven.

Robert May: *The Accomplisht Cook*

QUAKING PUDDING

4 egg yolks
2 egg whites
275 ml (1/2 pt) double cream
25 ml (1 1/2 tbls) flour
15 ml (1 tbls) rosewater
For the sauce:
30 ml (2 tbls) rosewater
30 ml (2 tbls) sugar
50 g (2 oz) butter
30 ml (2 tbls) water

Beat the egg yolks and whites into the cream, then beat in the flour and rosewater to form a thick batter. Rub a piece of butter into a thick pudding cloth to help it retain the batter. Support the cloth in a 575 ml (1 pt) basin, pour in the batter, tie the cloth securely, and plunge the pudding into a pan of boiling water. Simmer for 30 minutes, then remove from the pan and swiftly plunge into cold water. Turn the pudding out on to a warm plate. Make the sauce by melting the ingredients together, stirring constantly, and pour over the pudding.

Rebecca Price: *The Compleat Cook*

MARZIPAN BACON

To make Collops like Bacon of Marchpane: Take some of your Marchpane Paste and work it in red Saunders till it be red: then rowl a broad sheet of white Paste, and a sheet of red Paste, three of the white, and four of the red, and so one upon another in mingled sorts, every red between, then cut it overthwart, till it look like Collops of Bacon, then dry it.

225 g (8 oz) ground almonds
100 g (4 oz) caster sugar
30 ml (2 tbls) rosewater
red food colouring
cornflour or icing sugar for dusting

Beat the almonds and sugar with the rosewater to form a stiff paste. Divide in two, and knead a few drops of the red food colour into one half. Using either cornflour or icing sugar to dust the paste, roll out half the white mixture into a rectangle about 10 mm (¹/₂ in) in thickness, and the remainder into three thinner rectangles of the same size. Divide the red paste into four, and roll each piece out into similar rectangles. Starting with the thick white slab ('the fat'), build up alternate red and white layers to form a piece of 'streaky bacon', from which thin slices or 'collops' can then be cut and allowed to dry.

W.M.: *The Compleat Cook and Queen's Delight*, 1671 edition

SHROPSHIRE CAKES

To make a Shropshire cake: Take two pound of dryed flour after it has been searced fine, one pound of good sugar dried and searced, also a little beaten sinamon or some nottmegg greeted and steeped in rose water; so straine two eggs, whites and all, not beaten to it, as much unmelted butter as will work it to a paste: so mould it & roule it into longe rouses, and cutt off as much at a time as will make a cake, two ounces is enough for one cake: then roule it in a ball between your hands; so flat it on a little white paper cut for a cake, and with your hand beat it about as big as a cheese trancher and a little thicker than a past board: then prick them with a comb not too deep in squares like diamons and prick the cake in every diamon to the bottom; so take them in an oven not too hot: when they rise up white let them soake a little, then draw. If the sugar be dry enough you need not dry it but searce it: you must brake in your eggs after you have wroat in some of your butter into your flower: prick and mark them when they are cold: this quantity will make a dozen and two or three, which is enough for my own at a time: take off the paper when they are cold.

225 g (8 oz) butter
450 g (1 lb) flour
225 g (8 oz) caster sugar
1.5 ml (¹/₄ tsp) grated nutmeg
1 egg
5 ml (1 tsp) rosewater

Rub the butter into the dry ingredients, then work in the egg and rosewater to form a very stiff dough. Cut off lumps of dough, and work into 5 mm (¹/₄ in) thick cakes, 10 cm (4 in) in diameter. Using a comb, mark the top surface into diamonds, cutting half-way through the cake, then use a broad skewer to prick all the way through the centre of each diamond. Transfer to baking sheets, and bake for 20 minutes as gas mark 4, 180°C (350°F). Remove from the sheets with a metal spatula, and place on a wire tray to cool.

Madam Susanne Avery: *A Plain Plantain*

GEORGIAN RECIPES

PLAIN PUDDING

Puddings boiled or baked, sweet, plain or savoury, formed a major part of 18th-century fare. Plain pudding is simply pancake batter boiled in a cloth (plain and suet puddings are actually lighter when boiled in a cloth, because they can expand in all directions). The same batter baked in a tin under roasting meat becomes Yorkshire pudding. On 13 February 1757 Thomas Turner dined on hog's cheek and vegetables with a 'plain batter pudding', all boiled. Parson Woodforde regaled his parishioners on Tithe Audit-day 1799 with boiled and roast meat and plenty of plum and plain puddings. Mrs Raffald's pudding is simple to make, and very good.

50 g (2 oz) plain flour
1.5 ml (¼ tsp) salt
3 eggs
225 ml (8 fl oz) milk or single cream

For this size of pudding make a 45 cm (18 in) square pudding cloth of white cotton or doubled muslin. Boil a large pan of water and put an old plate in the bottom. Drop the pudding cloth in briefly, lift it out with a wooden spoon and let it drape over the spoon handle placed across a pan to drip. Have ready a piece of string. Sift the flour and salt into a bowl. In another bowl beat the eggs well. Add the flour, salt and milk and beat to make a thin batter. Squeeze out the pudding cloth, lay it on the table and sprinkle well with flour, gently shaking off the excess. To support the cloth while filling it, lay it in a basin with the floured side up, pour in the batter, gather up the corners and all the edges (leaving room for the pudding to expand), tie securely with string and place in a pan of boiling water, which must cover the pudding at all times. Cover the pan, leaving a small gap, and boil for 30 minutes. Lift the pudding out and dip briefly in cold water to loosen the cloth. Place in a colander, untie the string and peel back the cloth. Place a heated dish over the pudding, reverse the colander and gently peel away the rest of the cloth. Serve at once with meat, or as a dessert with hot wine sauce (*see* p 187).

Elizabeth Raffald:
The experienced English housekeeper

OYSTER LOAVES

Oysters were a favourite dish in the 18th century, and were often served as a garnish or sauce with meat. A common way of cooking them was to dip them in batter and deep-fry in lard. Oyster loaves make a pretty side dish for a first course.

4 underdone French rolls, each
weighing about 50 g (2 oz)
100 g (4 oz) butter, melted
12 small fresh oysters
30 ml (2 tbls) white wine
a pinch of grated nutmeg
a pinch of ground mace

Preheat the oven to gas mark 7, 220°C, 425°F. Cut the tops off the rolls and scoop out most of the middles. Brush the undersides of the lids and the hollows of the loaves with melted butter. Toast in the oven until lightly golden. Sauté the oysters in the remaining hot butter for 2–3 minutes or until the edges curl. Add the wine and spices to the pan. Put 3 oysters and a little sauce in each hot roll, replace the lids and serve at once.

Hannah Glasse:
The art of cookery made plain and easy

WHOLE FISH IN PASTRY

'Scale the Salmon, wash and dry him, chine him, and season him with Salt, Pepper, Ginger, Cloves, and Mace; lay him on a Sheet of Paste, and form it in the Shape of a Salmon, lay in Slices of Ginger, large Mace, and Butter upon the Fish, and turn up the other half of your Sheet of Paste on the Back, closing them on the Belly-side, from Head to Tail, bringing him into Proportion with Head, Fins, Gills, and Tail: Scale him, leave a Funnel to pour in Butter, and when it is bak'd, set it by to cool.'

1 whole fish, gutted and boned, but with head and tail left on, weighing about 450 g (1 lb)
salt and pepper
1.5 ml ($^1/_4$ tsp) ground mace
2.5 ml ($^1/_2$ tsp) ground ginger or grated fresh ginger root
40 g (1$^1/_2$ oz) butter, cut into slivers
450 g (1 lb) shortcrust or puff pastry
1 raisin
1 egg white
15 ml (1 tbls) top of the milk

Wash the fish and dry with absorbent paper. Season it inside with the salt, pepper, mace and ginger, and insert slivers of butter. Roll out the pastry into a long oval, 5 cm (2 in) longer at each end than the fish, making sure it is wide enough to fold over the fish, with a spare 2.5–5 cm (1–2 in) to seal it. Transfer the fish carefully on to the pastry and place on the bottom half of the oval, its belly towards you. Fold the pastry over, and trim off the excess. Seal with water and crimp the edge. Adjust the shape of the tail and head if necessary. Transfer the fish to a foil-covered baking sheet.

To make scales: roll out the pastry trimmings, cut out oval scales, and, beginning at the tail end, stick them on with water in an overlapping design. Make a gill and fins, and stick in a raisin for an eye. Beat the egg white and milk together, then drizzle it over the pastry from a brush (brushing would flatten the scales too much). Bake in the top part of the oven at gas mark 6, 200°C, 400°F for 10 minutes until beginning to colour, then move it to the middle for 10 minutes, after which reduce the heat to gas mark 4, 180°C, 350°F to bake for a further 20 minutes. (If the fish is short and thick give it 10 minutes longer.) Serve hot or cold with pickled or sliced lemons. The dish may be decorated with sprigs of flowers or herbs.

John Nott:
The cook's and confectioner's dictionary

ANCHOVIES WITH PARMESAN CHEESE

'To make a nice whet before dinner, or a side dish for a second course. Fry some bits of bread about the length of an anchovy in good oil or butter, lay the half of an anchovy, with the bone upon each bit, and strew over them some Parmesan cheese grated fine, and colour them nicely in an oven, or with a salamander, squeeze the juice of an orange or lemon, and pile them in your dish and send to the table. This seems to be but a trifling thing but I never saw it come whole from the table.'

Brown your anchovies in the oven, or under the grill. 'The half of an anchovy' means half a fish, or two modern tinned 'fillets'.

William Verral: *The cook's paradise*

SALAMANGUNDY

This magnificent salad was an opportunity for the cook to show her expertise in choosing a good balance of bland soft meats, sharp pickles, crisp vegetables and colourful leaves and flowers. Traditionally the ingredients were chopped small, and layered and heaped into a sugar-loaf shape, which mixed them all up together. This 1747 recipe reflects the new 'clean' taste in food: Mrs Glasse keeps each ingredient separate and recognisable in its own saucer, arranged on a large tray or platter, around a raised central dish. The spaces between the saucers are filled with watercress and flowers. The central raised dish is of chopped pickled herring. For the others you may choose a good balanced selection from the following:

cucumber, sliced very thin
apples, chopped small
onions, chopped small
celery, chopped small
crisp lettuce, finely shredded
peeled grapes
cooked French beans
pickled herring, chopped small
pickled gherkins, chopped small
pickled red cabbage
capers
lemons, sliced or chopped
anchovies
hard-boiled egg yolks
hard-boiled egg whites
cooked fowl, cut in strips or chopped

Hannah Glasse:
The art of cookery made plain and easy

BEETROOT PANCAKES

'A pretty corner dish for dinner or supper.'

175 g (6 oz) peeled cooked beetroot
30 ml (2 tbls) brandy
45 ml (3 tbls) double cream
4 egg yolks
30 ml (2 tbls) plain flour
10 ml (2 tsps) caster sugar
5 ml (1 tsp) grated nutmeg
clarified butter (*see* p 186)

Mash the beetroot as finely as possible and mix with the other ingredients (or put all into a blender). Heat a shallow layer of clarified butter in a frying pan. Drop the beetroot mixture from the point of a tablespoon into the butter and shake the pan to flatten if necessary. Turn down the heat, as these burn very easily. Turn the pancakes over – they will cook quickly. Wipe out the pan if necessary between batches. These unusual delicate pancakes are good hot or cold. 'Garnish with green sweetmeats, preserved apricots or green sprigs of myrtle.'

Elizabeth Raffald:
The experienced English housekeeper

STEWED RED CABBAGE

This is an incredibly easy and tasty dish – you just have to be prepared for blue sausages!

1 red cabbage, quartered and thinly
    sliced
450 g (1 lb) sausages
4–6 slices smoked bacon, chopped
275 ml (¹/₂ pt) consommé or gravy
salt and pepper

Put cabbage, sausages, bacon, consommé (or gravy) and seasoning into a large saucepan. Bring to the boil then cook over a gentle heat for about 30–40 minutes, stirring occasionally, until sausages are cooked through and cabbage is tender.

Hannah Glasse:
The art of cookery made plain and easy

CLARIFIED BUTTER

This is well worth doing. Once the buttermilk sediment has been removed from butter, it will keep indefinitely.

    Melt 450 g (1 lb) of unsalted butter gently in a saucepan and let the first foam subside. Pour through a coffee filter paper, or simply let it stand, then pour off the clear butter into a keeping basin. When cold, remove any buttermilk from the bottom.

MELTED BUTTER SAUCE

10 ml (2 tsps) plain flour
150 ml (¹/₄ pt) water
a pinch of salt
50–75 g (2–3 oz) butter

In a small pan mix the flour, water and salt. Stir over gentle heat, without allowing it to boil. When

hot, add the butter, cut into bits. Stir well until smooth. The sauce will not reheat, and if allowed to boil will taste raw. Sometimes a drop or two of lemon juice was added.

POTTED CHESHIRE CHEESE

This was a good way of improving a hard cheese and of preserving one that was about to go off. It actually improves with keeping.

225 g (8 oz) mature Cheshire cheese
50–75 g (2–3 oz) unsalted butter
30 ml (2 tbls) good sweet sherry
7 ml (1 rounded tsp) ground mace
clarified butter

Grate the cheese finely and mix with the butter, which should be soft but not melted. Add the sherry and mace, and mix well. Press well down in a pot, and cover with clarified butter.

Hannah Glasse:
The art of cookery made plain and easy

Port may be used in place of sherry. Eat sliced with walnuts and pears at the end of dinner.

WINE SAUCE

This was the most usual sauce for puddings.

225 ml (8 fl oz) wine
50 g (2 oz) butter
30 g (1¼ oz) caster sugar

Mix the ingredients together and heat. Serve in a hot sauceboat. Lemon juice can be substituted for the wine.

TEA CAUDLE

'Elegant enough for a supper table.'
Ale or wine caudles were traditional hot drinks, still taken at breakfast or supper until well into the 18th century. Tea caudle seems to be an innovation in the late 17th century when tea was first introduced from China. (Indian tea did not arrive until the 1830s.) Green China tea may be bought from specialist shops.

275 ml (½ pt) strong green China tea
15 ml (3 tsps) caster sugar
5 ml (1 tsp) grated nutmeg
1 egg yolk
125 ml (4 fl oz) white wine

Strain the tea into a small saucepan. Add the sugar and nutmeg and heat. In a small basin beat the egg yolk, add the wine and pour these into the hot tea, stirring continuously over gentle heat until very hot. Pour into a warmed caudle pot or china tea dishes.

Eliza Smith:
The compleat housewife, 1736 edition

Use the green tea leaves over again to make weak tea for drinking with slices of rich seed cake. Tea was so expensive that the leaves were often used twice.

PUNCH

A favourite 18th-century drink, brought from India in the late 17th century by merchants of the East India Company.

1.1 l (2 pt) claret
275 ml (½ pt) brandy
grated nutmeg, sugar and lemon juice
toast, to serve

Mix the ingredients and serve in a punchbowl with toasted bread floating on the top. A variation of this was milk punch, where milk replaces the wine.

A HEDGEHOG
(not a real one!)

225 g (8 oz) ground almonds
15 ml (1 tbls) sweet sherry
5 ml (1 tsp) orange flower water
3 egg yolks
2 egg whites
150 ml (¼ pt) double cream
85 g (3 oz) granulated sugar
50 g (2 oz) butter
2 cloves or currants
100 g (4 oz) blanched almonds,
    thinly sliced lengthwise

Place all ingredients except the cloves or currants and sliced almonds in a large saucepan and mix together. Cook over a gentle heat, stirring constantly, until the mixture thickens sufficiently to hold its shape. Turn the mixture out onto a large plate and form into the shape of a hedgehog. Add eyes using cloves or currants, and spines using the chopped almonds. Surround the hedgehog with a sauce such as custard, or stewed fruit such as damsons, or apples cooked in red wine.

Hannah Glasse:
The art of cookery made plain and easy

STRAWBERRY FRITTERS

Plain fritters, made of ale, flour and eggs, were often eaten, but especially at Easter.

450 g (1 lb) large dry strawberries
150 g (6 oz) plain flour
50 g (2 oz) caster sugar
10 ml (2 tsps) grated nutmeg
2 eggs, well beaten
225 ml (8 fl oz) single cream
lard for deep-frying
sugar, to finish

The strawberries must be dry. Leave the stalks on for easier handling. Sift the flour into a bowl and add the caster sugar and nutmeg. Make a well and drop in the eggs and cream. Then stir until all the flour and sugar are assimilated. Let the batter stand an hour or two. Dip each strawberry in batter until it is completely coated, and fry a few at a time in hot lard. Your lard must be hot enough to puff them, but not so hot as to brown them too quickly. Drain on absorbent paper and keep hot. Pile them in a pyramid in a hot dish and sprinkle sugar over. Decorate with leaves.

William Verral: The cook's paradise

RICH SEED CAKE

Caraway seeds were enormously popular in the later 18th century. This rich cake would be eaten at breakfast or afternoon tea among the gentry and middle classes. It was thought that the longer cakes were beaten the better – Mrs Raffald recommends beating this cake for 2 hours. Modern baking powder was not invented until the mid-19th century, so the success of a cake like this lies in its very careful technique. All ingredients and bowls must be slightly warmer than room temperature. Assemble all the ingredients before you begin, prepare the tin and preheat the oven.

225 g (8 oz) plain flour
5 ml (1 tsp) grated nutmeg
5 ml (1 tsp) grated cinnamon
25 g (1 oz) caraway seeds
225 g (8 oz) unsalted butter,
  softened
225 g (8 oz) caster sugar
4 eggs, separated, tepid

Line and grease a 20 cm (8 in) diameter, 7.5 cm (3 in) deep cake tin. Sift the flour and spices into a bowl, and add the caraway seeds. Make sure your mixing bowl is big enough, and slightly warm. Cream the butter and sugar in it very thoroughly, scraping the sides of the bowl. In a warm jug, beat the tepid egg yolks very well, then add the creamed mixture gradually, beating very well after each addition. With a scrupulously clean beater, beat the egg whites until they are stiff but not dry. Using a metal tablespoon, fold the beaten whites and the flour into the creamed mixture, about a fifth at a time; fold in by slicing the spoon edge gently down the middle, lifting and turning as lightly as possible, at the same time turning the bowl slowly with your other hand. The flour should be shaken in gently from a height. Stop as soon as the mixture appears amalgamated. Empty gently into the prepared tin and fork roughly level. Bake in the middle of the oven at gas mark 3, 170°C, 325°F for 1½ hours. Cool in the tin for 10 minutes, then turn on to a wire rack and remove the papers. The cake will be delicately crisp on the outside, and inside will have a light crumbly texture.

Elizabeth Raffald:
The experienced English housekeeper

VICTORIAN RECIPES

POULET SAUTÉ À LA PLOMBIÈRE

A decorative hot entrée for a formal dinner in 1895 which would make a practical main dish by itself today.

2 small chickens, about 900 g
  (2 lb) each
100 g (4 oz) streaky bacon
50 g (2 oz) unsalted butter
2 shallots, finely chopped
15 ml (1 tbls) flour
15 ml (1 tbls) mild curry powder
10 ml (2 tsps) desiccated coconut
125 ml (4 fl oz) white wine
15 ml (1 tbls) brandy
575 ml (1 pt) white stock
4 parsley sprigs and $^1/_2$ bay leaf, tied
  in muslin
salt and pepper
a pinch of grated nutmeg
5 ml (1 tsp) redcurrant jelly
juice of $^1/_2$ sour orange
175 g (6 oz) long grain rice
a little extra stock (optional)

To garnish:
rind of $^1/_2$ orange, pared thinly and cut
  into matchsticks
6–8 warm fleurons (half-moons) of
  cooked puff pastry

Joint the chickens and dice the bacon, discarding any rind. Melt the butter in a saucepan or flameproof casserole. Fry the bacon for about 2 minutes, shaking the pan, then add the chicken pieces and shallots, and sauté until lightly browned on all sides. Mix together the flour, curry powder and coconut and sprinkle over the chicken. Stir round, and pour in the wine, brandy and stock. Add the herb bundle, then bring to the boil and add the seasoning, nutmeg, redcurrant jelly and orange juice. Reduce the heat and simmer, uncovered until the chicken pieces are tender. While the meat is simmering, cook the rice in boiling, salted water until tender, then drain and keep warm. Skim off any fat from the curry sauce, remove the herb bundle, and thin with a little extra stock if wished. Simmer the shreds of orange rind in water for 2 minutes and then drain. Arrange the rice in a circle, pile the chicken, bacon and sauce in the centre, and garnish.

Charles Herman Senn: *Recherché Cookery*

CALF'S FOOT JELLY

Chefs and good cooks still considered it necessary to make calf's foot jelly, not only as nourishment for invalids, but as by far and away the best basis for their many (often elaborate) jellied desserts. Isinglass was accepted as an alternative but was less esteemed. Gelatine, made by boiling hooves and hides, came into its own when the first cheap jellies became an 'instant' success at the Great Exhibition of 1851, but made any high-class cook wince.

To make 'jelly stock': 'Take two calfs' feet, cut them up and boil in three quarts of water; as soon as it boils remove it to the corner of the fire, and simmer for five hours, keeping it skimmed, pass through a hair sieve into a basin, and let it remain until quite hard, then remove the oil and fat, and wipe the top dry. Place in a stewpan one gill of water, one of sherry, half a pound of lump sugar, the juice of four lemons, the rinds of two, and the whites and shells of five eggs, whisk until the sugar is melted, then add the jelly, place it on the fire, and whisk until boiling, pass it through a jelly-bag, pouring that back again which comes through first until quite clear; it is then ready for use, by putting it in moulds or glasses.'

Alexis Soyer:
The Modern Housewife or Ménagère

MACARONI À LA REINE

Miss Acton's 'excellent and delicate mode of dressing macaroni' makes delightful reading but long-winded instruction. Its essentials in modern terms are these.

225 g (8 oz) macaroni
275 g (10 oz) white Stilton or other
  rich white quick-melting cheese
  without rind (see note)
50 g (2 oz) unsalted butter
350 ml (12 fl oz) double cream or
  thick rich white sauce
salt and pepper
a good pinch of ground mace
a pinch of cayenne pepper
fried breadcrumbs, finely crushed

Cook the macaroni in boiling salted water until tender, then drain. While it is cooking, flake the cheese and the butter. Heat the cream or sauce almost to boiling point. Add the cheese and butter in small portions, with salt, pepper, mace and cayenne, and stir until dissolved. Pour over the hot, drained macaroni, and toss to mix. Turn into a warmed serving dish, and sprinkle thickly with golden crumbs before serving.

Eliza Acton: *Modern Cookery for Private Families*, 1874 edition

Miss Acton suggests using Stilton without the blue mould. Perhaps young Stiltons were less blued in those days.

PHEASANT GITANA

Weekend shooting and house parties were a feature of upper-class Victorian life. This was a useful way to handle a badly shot bird for formal dining.

1 pheasant, trussed
225 g (8 oz) streaky bacon, rinded
  and cut into 2.5 cm (1 in) squares
25 g (1 oz) butter
1 garlic clove
2 large Spanish onions, sliced
4 ripe tomatoes, sliced
150 ml (¼ pt) sherry
5 ml (1 tsp) paprika

Put the pheasant in a large flameproof casserole with the bacon, butter and garlic. Fry, turning the pheasant, until it is browned all over. Pour off excess fat, then add the onions, tomatoes and sherry. Cover and simmer for 45–60 minutes until the pheasant is tender, shaking the pan occasionally. Just before serving, stir in the paprika.

Charles Elmé Francatelli: *The Cook's Guide and Housekeeper's and Butler's Assistant*

Gertie Gitana was a popular star of Victorian music halls.

STEWED TROUT

A 19th-century cook had no frozen, farmed and supermarket trout, only river fish which might be much larger if old and wily. The cooking time below has been adapted to suit both; otherwise the author's tasty recipe is almost unchanged.

2 medium-sized trout
75 g (3 oz) butter
15 ml (1 tbls) flour
a good pinch of ground mace
a good pinch of grated nutmeg
a pinch of cayenne pepper
425 ml (³/₄ pt) veal or chicken stock
3 parsley sprigs
1 bay leaf
1 broad strip lemon peel, rolled
salt
30 ml (2 tbls) dry white wine
    (optional)

Clean the fish, and trim the tails and fins; remove heads if you wish. Rinse inside and pat quite dry. Melt the butter in a large deep frying pan or skillet. Stir in the flour, mace, nutmeg and cayenne together. Add the trout, and brown them on both sides, shaking the pan to prevent them sticking. Now add the stock, parsley, bay leaf, lemon peel, salt and wine if using. Half-cover the pan, and reduce the heat to a gentle simmer. Cook for 15–35 minutes depending on the size of the fish. When ready, the fish should be tender when pierced with a thin skewer, but not soft enough to break up. Remove the fish to a warmed serving dish. Skim all the fat off the cooking liquid, and strain some or all of it over the fish. Serve at once.

Eliza Acton:
Modern Cookery for Private Families

RICE À LA SOEUR NIGHTINGALE
(Sister Nightingale's Rice)

175 g (6 oz) long grain rice
salt and pepper
450 g (1 lb) smoked haddock fillet
2 square slices bread, crusts removed
75–100 g (3–4 oz) unsalted butter
3 hard-boiled eggs
a pinch of grated nutmeg
15 ml (1 tbls) Parmesan cheese,
    grated

Cook the rice in plenty of boiling, salted water until tender. While the rice is cooking, pour boiling water over the haddock, and leave to stand for 5 minutes. Drain the rice when ready. Cut each bread slice into four triangles. Fry in 40 g (1¹/₂ oz) of the butter until golden on both sides. Remove with a fish slice, leaving any fat in the pan. Drain on absorbent paper, then keep warm. Separate the whites and yolks of the hard-boiled eggs into separate bowls. Chop the whites. Remove any bones and skin from the fish and flake the flesh coarsely. Mix with the chopped egg whites. Add the remaining butter to the frying pan and toss the rice in it over a gentle heat, adding seasoning and nutmeg to taste. Mix in the fish and egg white mixture, and pile in a pyramid on a hot dish. Sieve the egg yolks and cheese together, and sprinkle over the mixture. Put in the oven at gas mark 4, 180°C (350°F) for 4–5 minutes until the cheese begins to colour. Add the triangles of fried bread and serve at once.

Charles Elmé Francatelli:
*The Cook's Guide and
Housekeeper's and Butler's Assistant*

POOR MAN'S SOUP

Alexis Soyer's soup kitchen meal for the starving was widely publicised and copied. Although only slightly more nourishing than other soup handouts which he condemned, it did a lot to jolt the consciences of the affluent who accepted his flamboyant (and sometimes specious) arguments and appeal to them.

50 g (2 oz) dripping
100 g (4 oz) meat cut into 2.5 cm
  (1 in) dice
100 g (4 oz) onions, thinly sliced
100 g (4 oz) turnips, cut into small
  dice ('the peel will do')
50 g (2 oz) leeks, thinly sliced ('the
  green tops will do')
75 g (3 oz) celery
350 g (12 oz) wholemeal flour
225 g (8 oz) pearl barley
75 g (3 oz) salt
7 g ($^1/_4$ oz) brown sugar
9 l (2 gals) water

'I first put two ounces of dripping in a saucepan (capable of holding two gallons of water), with a quarter of a pound of leg of beef without bones cut into squares of about an inch; and two middling-sized onions, peeled and sliced; I then set the saucepan over a coal fire, and stirred the contents round for a few minutes with a wooden (or iron) spoon until fried lightly brown. I had then ready washed the peelings of two turnips, fifteen green leaves or tops of celery, and the green part of two leeks; (the whole of which, I must observe, are always thrown away). Having cut the above vegetables into small pieces, I threw them into the saucepan with the other ingredients, stirring them occasionally over the fire for another ten minutes; then added one quart of cold water and three quarters of a pound of common flour and half a pound of pearl barley, mixing all well together; I then added seven quarts of hot water, seasoned with three ounces

of salt, and a quarter of an ounce of brown sugar, stirred occasionally until boiling, and allowed to simmer very gently for three hours; at the end of which time I found the barley perfectly tender... The above soup has been tasted by numerous noblemen, members of parliament, and several ladies who have lately visited my kitchen department and who have considered it very good and nourishing ... As regards the peelings and ends of vegetables which I use in my receipts, it is a well-known fact that the exteriors of every vegetable, roots in particular, contains more flavour than the interior of it ... It will be perceived that I have omitted all kinds of spice except in those dishes which are intended expressly for them, as I consider they only flatter the appetite and irritate the stomach and make it crave for more food; my object being not to create an appetite but to satisfy it.'

Alexis Soyer: *Soyer's Charitable Cookery or the Poor Man's Regenerator*

Other root vegetables, such as carrots, can also be used and a thicker, more stew-like dish is created with less water.

SAVOY CAKE

A grand dinner party or banquet always featured large and small cakes, especially Savoy cake, among its sweet entremets or desserts. Since stale Savoy cake was also the basis of creamy desserts such as Coburg pudding and trifle, a shrewd chef included these in his menu too. This is Alexis Soyer's basic Savoy cake, probably made, as was common, in a fancy mould rather like a jelly mould. Hot steamed and similar puddings were also made in fancy moulds so that they looked elaborately carved when turned out.

clarified butter
225 g (8 oz) caster sugar, plus a little extra
1–2 drops lemon essence
7 eggs, separated
75 g (3 oz) plain flour
75 g (3 oz) potato flour

Brush the inside of a 2.5 l (4¹/₂ pt) decorative mould or a 20 cm (8 in) diameter, 7.5 cm (3 in) deep cake tin with clarified butter. Invert it to drain. When the butter has set, sprinkle the inside of the mould or tin liberally with caster sugar, and shake out the excess. Add the lemon essence to the caster sugar, then beat with the egg yolks in a large bowl until thick and almost white. Separately, whisk the egg whites until stiff but not dry. Mix the plain and potato flour and sift a little into the egg yolk mixture, folding it in with a metal spoon. Fold in about half the egg whites, then sift and fold in about half the remaining flour mixture. Repeat, using all the ingredients. Using a spatula, turn the mixture into the prepared mould or tin as lightly as possible. Bake at gas mark 4, 180°C (350°F) for 1–1¹/₄ hours. Test for readiness by running a hot thin skewer into the cake. Turn out to cool on a wire rack. (Leave for 1–2 days before cutting up to make into a dessert.)

Alexis Soyer:
The Modern Housewife or Ménagère

PETITES BOUCHÉES

These little pastries were offered among Victorian sweet entremets or desserts at formal dinners and evening parties.

175 g (6 oz) whole almonds
100 g (4 oz) caster sugar
rind of ¹/₂ lemon, pared thinly
1 egg white
275 g (10 oz) puff pastry

Blanch the almonds by plunging them in boiling water for about 3 minutes, then rub off the skins and chop very finely. Pound together the sugar and lemon rind in a mortar, then sift to remove any solid rind. Mix in the almonds. Beat the egg white until liquid, and mix into the almonds and sugar to make a paste (you may not need it all). Roll out the puff pastry to a thickness of 5 mm (¹/₄ in) and cut into diamonds, rounds, ovals, etc. Re-roll and recut trimmings. Spread the pastry shapes thickly with the almond paste. Bake at gas mark 6, 200°C (400°F) until gilded. Cool on a wire rack.

Mrs Isabella Beeton:
The Book of Household Management, 1866

BAVARIAN CREAMS

Soyer, in The Modern Housewife, *explains how these 'creams' can be flavoured like jellies with ripe fruit in syrup or preserves. He gives a basic recipe for a plain one, using generous Victorian quantities. It has been adapted for modern use.*

1 vanilla pod, split
575 ml (1 pt) milk
5 egg yolks
175 g (6 oz) caster sugar
45 ml (3 tbls) any sweet liqueur
25 g (1 oz) gelatine
425 ml (³/₄ pt) whipping cream

Simmer the vanilla pod in the milk for 10 minutes. Meanwhile, beat the egg yolks and sugar together in a saucepan until thick and quite white. Still beating, add the hot milk gradually and place over a low heat until the custard thickens. Strain into a bowl and cool. While cooling, heat the liqueur in a small pan until very hot; sprinkle in the gelatine little by little and stir until it dissolves. Do not allow to boil. Stir it into the cooling custard and chill until the mixture begins to thicken up at the edges. While chilling, whip the cream fairly stiffly. Fold it into the thickening custard. Pour into a wetted 1.7 l (3 pt) ornamental mould and leave for at least 2 hours. Turn out on to a chilled serving dish.

Alexis Soyer:
The Modern Housewife or Ménagère

D'ARTOIS OF APRICOT

Both chefs and domestic cooks gave similar recipes for these popular little pastries; Francatelli's is one of the clearest. The only changes in the recipe below are one or two ideas from Victorian cook books, suggesting, for instance, a size for the d'artois.

450 g (1 lb) puff pastry
apricot jam
1 well-beaten egg mixed with a few
  drops of water
caster sugar

Take one-third of the pastry, and roll it out on a lightly floured surface into an oblong which will just fit on to a baking sheet about 35x30 cm (14x12 in) in size. You could use a standard 35x25 cm (14x10 in) Swiss roll tin turned upside down. Lay the pastry on the tin. Spread a thick even layer of apricot jam over the pastry to within 2.5 cm (1 in) of the edge. Brush the edge with beaten egg, using a brush dipped in cold water. Roll out the remaining pastry to fit the first sheet. Lay it over it, and press down the edges to seal. With the back of a knife, mark the pastry into small oblongs about 7.5 cm (3 in) long and 2.5 cm (1 in) wide. Brush evenly all over with egg. Using a small knife, flick up tiny nicks of pastry in rows, making a kind of feather pattern on each cake. Bake at gas mark 6, 200°C (400°F) for 15–20 minutes. When risen and golden brown, sprinkle evenly with sugar. Return to the oven for 2–3 minutes to melt it, then place under a moderate grill for a moment or two to glaze. Cool and cut into oblongs. To serve, arrange a row in a circle on a doily, place another on top, then another until all are arranged.

Charles Elmé Francatelli: *The Cook's Guide
and Housekeeper's and Butler's Assistant*

RECIPE INDEX

ACKNOWLEDGEMENTS

The publishers would like to thank Shirley Walsh (aka Sosia Juncina); Historic Haut Cuisine; Lace Wars 18th-century Re-enactment Group, Janet Tattersley, Rob Richardson and Val Horsler for cooking and presenting a number of recipes featured in this book, and James O. Davies and Peter Williams for photographing them. We also appreciate the help of Adèle Campbell who read and commented on the text.

The publishers would like to thank the following people and organisations listed below for permission to reproduce the photographs in this book. Every care has been taken to trace copyright holders, but any omissions will, if notified, be corrected in any future edition.

All photographs are © English Heritage.NMR with the exception of the following:
Bodleian Library, University of Oxford DOUCE P.412 p46; British Library p32 (Add. 42130 f.163v), p82 (Add. 42130 f.206v), p114 (Roy. 14.E.IV f.265v); Bridgeman Art Library p19 (Museo della Civilta Romana, Rome, Italy, Giraudon), p49 (Private Collection/The Stapleton Collection), p60 (Courtesy of the Warden and Scholars of New College, Oxford), p77 (Musee des Antiquites Nationales, St. Germain-en-Laye, France, Archives Charmet), p126 (Museum of London, UK); Cotswold Farm Park, Guiting Power, Gloucestershire p15; Crown copyright.NMR pp25, 99; Mary Evans Picture Library pp21, 69, 70; National Trust Photographic Library pp92, 108 (Nadia Mackenzie), p139 (Andreas von Einsiedel); Andrew Tyner p83.

Line illustrations by Peter Brears